The Teacher's Guide for A Treasury of Sephardic Laws and Customs

The Teacher's Guide for A Treasury of Sephardic Laws and Customs

Rabbi Herbert C. Dobrinsky, Ed.D.

YESHIVA UNIVERSITY PRESS, INC.
NEW YORK, NEW YORK

KTAV PUBLISHING HOUSE, INC.
HOBOKEN, NEW JERSEY

1988

Published in memory of

Dr. Samuel Belkin ע"ה
Rachel Ades ע"ה
Salvo R. Arias ע"ה
Dr. Benjamin Brickman ע"ה
H. Jerome Sisselman ע"ה
Dr. Solomon Skaist ע"ה

The author and Yeshiva University gratefully acknowledge with sincere thanks the generous grant in memory of Salvo R. Arias, of blessed memory, by his beloved wife, Hilda B. Arias, and his devoted children Robert and Louise Arias, which has made the publication of this *Teacher's Guide* possible.

Contents

SECTION I

SECTION II

SECTION III

Introduction

America has long been noted as the "cultural potpourri" of the world, a position which, for us Jews, has become more effectively operative during the past four decades and more in the State of Israel. The notion of a pluralistic society, where each group brings the richness and the best of its uniqueness to contribute to the overall melding and strengthening of a land and its cultural, social, and educational experiences, reflects the quintessence of democratic living in a democratic society. To this dimension of creating a society, wherein these precepts are germane to the existence of the country and its credo, America stands unparalleled.

In a sense, this social dynamic may well be the time-hallowed contribution of Judaism to Western civilization. We have come to understand for ourselves and have successfully communicated to others our intrinsic belief in Monotheism and that there are many corridors which lead to the Heavenly Palace where man awaits Divine Judgment. For the Jews, this acceptance is achieved through the living of a noble life patterned after a tradition which has been our legacy and heritage for more than thirty-five hundred years. And yet, the concept has allowed for a diversity of expression within the acceptable norms of the Divine Law ofttimes expressed by the echo which was heard from on high when the divergent interpretations of Hillel and Shammai were at apparent loggerheads—"Both are the words of the One Living God."[1]

If this is true of opposing views in the interpretation of a given point of the Talmudic Law, much more so is this "unity in diversity" applicable to the development of different historical societies and communities which have developed over the millennia in different geographic areas, all serving to worship the One God of the One People of Israel through His One Torah. Thus, the development of an educational approach to the expounding, observance, and furtherance of Torah life by Sephardim and Ashkenazim in somewhat different styles is more accepted than might be expected.

Sephardic educational patterns were formulated as a result of the influence of the Golden Age in Spain, the great philosophers, poets, grammarians, exegetes, and philologists who studied the Bible, the Prophets, and the Hagiographa in their own particular manner, influenced perhaps by the Muslim environment in which they resided and inspired by the zeal of the wide range of general studies which were part of the milieu in which they flourished.[2]

This study is limited to the study of Sephardic customs especially as relates to the communities of Syria, Morocco, the Judeo-Spanish communities of the Balkans and Levant, and the Spanish and Portuguese, who originate from Amsterdam.

The dispersion of the Jewish people and the loss of contact between the communities caused each group to develop in its own way without too much communication with the other Jewish centers of learning, except for the occasional exchange of rabbinic responsa among the great halakhic authorities, who held opposing views as often as they were in accord with one another. Thus, an abyss of ignorance divided the Sephardic and Ashkenazic worlds, even as it often caused great gaps between groups within their own sphere. The Spanish and Portuguese Jews, after the expulsion from Spain in 1492, and from Portugal in 1496, made their way to different lands.[3] Those who ended up in Amsterdam led a different life from those who went to Turkey or North Africa. The same is true of Ashkenazic groups in France, Germany, and in other parts of the world. The one force which kept the Jews together within their own locality was the observance of the *halakhah* (Jewish law) in accordance with the particular *minhag* (custom) of the locality.[4]

The rabbinic responsa in each community deal with *halakhah* and *minhag* as the living and dynamic forces of religious expression responding to the inquiries of the masses. Thus, each community had its own sages and responsa, most of which is unknown, some of which is lost, but much of which remains as living testimony to the timeless Torah heritage which has continued to be passed from one generation to the other without serious disruption. Sephardic education, therefore, is the transmittal from one generation to the next of the unique interpretations of Torah life which grandfathers handed over to their sons, who then passed them on inviolate to their children in each period. For Sephardic Jewry to survive, this process must continue. To a large extent, the school or yeshiva will have to assume the surrogate role of parent in preserving that heritage, as is true of the schools of the Jewish people everywhere. "*Veshinantam lebanekha*" (Deuteronomy 6:7) is fulfilled by the school (and hopefully also by the parents) and will preserve the identity of each of their beautiful customs, which, together, formulate the panorama of Mosaic law.

An unfortunate lack of knowledge of the great sages who existed, wrote, and expounded the laws in Syria, Morocco, the Levantine and Balkan countries, and in other parts of the world since the period of the expulsion, has led many Ashkenazim and Sephardim alike to sense a spiritual impoverishment. The responsa, the laws and customs as taught and lived in these communities, are the major weapons whereby the battle can be won to restore the prestige of Jewish scholarship and the richness and nobility of Jewish life as expressed in all these countries, for the Jews in Israel, in North America, in Europe, and elsewhere, to better appreciate and understand. This study is written primarily to begin, in some small way, to pave the way to reestablish the glory of that multifaceted jewel called Sephardic Jewry, in its totality, so that its brightness may be reaffirmed and its glittering enlightenment may bring new understanding, respect, and added strength to Klal Yisrael—the entire Jewish people.

The first step, therefore, is to outline in even the most basic terms what the uninterrupted tradition of each of these communities has been and continues to be. While this effort will fall short of perfection because of the limitations of the time allocated to the study and the ability to accumulate the widest possible variety of usages from many more scholars, it nevertheless will point the way and fill a gap which has existed in English-speaking countries for many years. Jews must learn to be proud of their own tradition as handed down by their own fathers. Ashkenazim should not seek to transform Sephardim where they are the minority, nor should Sephardim seek to do the same where their numbers abound. We all have one God, one Torah, but each of us can express that love of God in our distinctive ways. The problem is that most fail to offer that expression of observance to God in any form.

A review of the history of the Sephardim (which is completely beyond the purview of this study) will enhance the appreciation of teacher and student alike for the nuances of the particular traditions to be found in the various communities. This study makes no pretense of being an historical or sociological work about the communities represented. The Bibliography provides ample samplings of excellent works which can be studied to gain these important insights and this essential understanding of Jewish history in its totality, as well as the position of Sephardim as compared with Ashkenazim in the different countries and societies.

A Treasury of Sephardic Laws and Customs: The Ritual Practices of Syrian, Moroccan, Judeo-Spanish, and Spanish and Portuguese Jewry will help each of the groups studied and described to have a fuller understanding of their own unique heritage. Hopefully, they will take the time and interest to discover the beauty of the practices of their fellow Sephardim and Ashkenazim as well. For, if we are all one people, although we need not express our worship in one uniform way, we must remember that "the Lord God of Israel is One God," and we, each of us, are the conveyors of that timeless belief which from the time of our Patriarch Abraham until today has helped improve the lot of mankind—while yet leaving much to be achieved until the ultimate prophecy will be fulfilled when all the nations of the world shall proclaim, "And on that day, the Lord God shall be One and His name shall be One" (Zekhariah 14:9).

An Overview of American Sephardic Jewry

The first Jews arrived in North America in 1654. Almost all of these twenty-three were Sephardim, refugees from Recife, Brazil.[5] Sephardim are Jews who migrated from Spain (Sepharad) to Holland and other countries of Western Europe and elsewhere. They are distinguished from Ashkenazim (often called "Yiddishim" by Sephardim, since most of them speak

Yiddish, which has a German base and is interspersed with a melange of Hebrew, Slavic languages, etc.), who are Jews who lived in Central and Eastern Europe, such as Germany, Russia, Poland, Czechoslovakia, Hungary, and Rumania. For the purposes of this study, all non-Ashkenazi Jews (except Yemenites) are treated as Sephardim. The history of the Sephardim is diverse and complex and took them to lands throughout the world from the time of the Spanish expulsion until today. They constitute a small but significant segment of the North American community in our times, and their cultural and religious heritage is seriously threatened as regards survival and self-perpetuation. For the technical student, the term *Sephardim* refers only to those Jews who originate from the Iberian Peninsula (i.e., Spain or Portugal).[6] However, since these Jews later made their way to the Balkan, North African, Levantine, and Middle Eastern Countries, as well as to Europe and the Americas, we shall speak of them all as Sephardim (in contradistinction to Ashkenazim, and to the Yemenites [who do not wish to be identified as Sephardim]).

Current Status of Sephardim in North America

Listing continents and regions in alphabetical order, but countries according to probable order of population size, the various groups of Sephardim who currently reside in North America derive from *Africa,* Morocco, Egypt, Tunisia, Algeria, Libya; *Asia,* Syria, Iraq, Iran, India, Lebanon, Afghanistan; *Asia Minor,* Turkey; *Asian Russia,* Bukhara; *Europe,* Turkey, Rhodes, Yugoslavia, Greece, Bulgaria, Holland, Great Britain, Georgia, Italy, Rumania. These communities of origin comprise the native lands of the total population of Sephardi Jews in the United States and Canada, who number between 200,000 and 250,000.[7] We have consciously omitted Israel, since most of the Sephardic Israeli emigrants stem from the above-described countries of origin in which they resided before they, or their families, came to Israel. The same holds true for the South American Sephardim in our midst.

Sephardim in North America have, for the most part, maintained their own religious institutions and cultural organizations distinct and apart from the general Jewish community, although in recent years (especially since the founding of the State of Israel), they have often joined forces with Ashkenazim on behalf of the State of Israel and other matters of worldwide concern to the Jewish world. Economically, the Sephardim can be said to have attained success on a comparable basis with that of their North American Ashkenazi brethren, many of whom also came to these shores after the turn of the twentieth century.[8]

The majority of Sephardim in North America still reside within the Greater New York metropolitan area, which contains the largest Judeo-Spanish-speaking (Ladino) community in the world, and is the largest center of Syrian (Arabic-speaking) Jews, both groups originally coming to America from the early 1900's until 1923.[9] Other large Sephardic communities are continuing to grow in California, Washington, Illinois, Florida, and Massachusetts. In Canada during the past twenty-five years, the North African and Middle Eastern French-speaking groups have settled in Montreal (25,000), and the Spanish-speaking (as well as French-speaking) North Africans have made their homes in Toronto (10,000). These groups continue to increase in number each year and have made their way as far west as Vancouver, British Columbia.

The threat to the spiritual and ethnic survival of Sephardic Jewry in North America (a "minority within a minority") is even more severe than the overriding concern described in the *Midstream* article (October, 1977), "The American Jewish Population Erosion," by Elihu Bergman, which describes the assimilation and intermarriage of the "vanishing American Jew."[10] For Sephardim, in addition to the rampant threat of *intermarriage* with non-Jews, *intramarriage* with Ashkenazim also presents a challenge to the survival of their distinctive cultural heritage, which, if lost, would weaken the fabric of overall Jewish life.[11] Throughout the ages, the two approaches to Halakhah and Jewish custom have added strength and beauty to the mosaic of Jewish living.

Relatively recent studies conducted in New York and Montreal, respectively, showed intermarriage at the alarming rate of 24 percent among Spanish-speaking Jews, and at one time, rising all the way to 61 percent, among Quebec's French-speaking Jews.[12] In contrast, the Syrian community has contained its intermarriage rate with non-Jews to well under 5 percent,[13] with some claiming it to be less than 1 percent. It is indeed significant that the Syrian community has some 90 percent of its children attending Hebrew day schools.[14] The prohibition by the Brooklyn Syrian rabbinate against the acceptance of any converts to Judaism (except for adoption purposes) is cited as another major cause for their strong group identity and the low rate of intermarriage.

The lack of educational material about the history, heritage, and cultural contributions of the respective Sephardic communities to the Jewish people is alarming and leaves those schools which do exist without the tools to do their jobs. Many of the available books relating to Sephardim derive from the period prior to, and following, the expulsion of the Jews from Spain and Portugal in 1492 and 1496. The valuable contributions of rabbinic scholarship developed during the past four hundred years have largely been neglected, although the Sephardim did indeed contribute many creative works to bolster their thriving Jewish life in their various communities during that period.[15] Regretfully, much of that treasure has been lost. Therefore, the quest for roots among Sephardim today is frantic, especially in the face of an Ashkenazic majority outside the State of Israel. Although many Sephardim readily adapted economically and were able to become acculturated in America, some lost much of their Sephardic ritual and the depth and widespread commitment to Jewish religious life in the process of acculturation and Americanization. The establishment of Jewish educational institutions was not a priority for the new immigrants when they arrived in the early 1900's and had to struggle to establish themselves. Their few schools were inadequate, understaffed, undisciplined, erratically attended, and had a curriculum which was antiquated.[16]

Indeed, it was only the Syrian community that succeeded in great measure in the field of Jewish education, and it was an uphill battle for them as well. However, their persistence bore fruit. Today, there are a good number of Syrian Yeshibot in Brooklyn, New York, Deal, New Jersey, and Los Angeles,

California. Regretfully, there is not yet one yeshiva for the Judeo-Spanish-speaking group in America, nor for any of the other Sephardic groups. In Canada, the North Africans have several schools in Montreal and in Toronto.

In recognition of the critical need for higher education on Sephardic Jewry, as early as 1964, Yeshiva University, then under the inspiring leadership of its late President, Dr. Samuel Belkin, of blessed memory, who together with The Haham, Rabbi Dr. Solomon Gaon, Chief Rabbi of the Sephardic Jews of the British Commonwealth, and with the help and leadership of the author, initiated the Sephardic Studies Program, which was the first college-level program of its kind in the world. It was established to help preserve the rich Sephardic heritage and to train rabbis, teachers, and other key leaders for the Sephardic Jewish community.[17] This was a pioneering effort in the crucial battle to restore a heritage in whose debt all Jewry stands.[18] The accumulated neglect of years has visibly spiritually impoverished the bearers of a noble and rich tradition. There are fortunately some serious Sephardic scholars and lay leaders who are eager to recapture the spirit of that time-hallowed, sacred tradition which first brought Judaism to America. The author, was professionally involved in the initiation of that program, and thereby became aware of the critical educational needs of the total Sephardic community throughout the United States and Canada.[19]

Nature of the Problem

The problem of the "vanishing American Jew" in the general North American Jewish community is enough of a threat to justifiably preoccupy the minds of the Jewish community's serious leaders. However, for the "minority" Sephardic Jewish community in America, the problem is even more frightening. As Sephardim mingle with the Ashkenazic majority and with non-Jews, their group identity is constantly challenged.[20] It becomes increasingly difficult for them to remain within the confines of their own relatively small groups or to perpetuate their groups' values and culture. And yet, the anomaly which captures the student of Sephardic life is that very strong kinship these various Sephardim sense towards their own groups. Despite their lack of numbers and knowledge, they take genuine pride in their Sephardi identity.[21] This wonderful sense of mutuality will diminish if they do not bolster it with profound understanding of their distinctive history and practical knowledge of their distinguishing characteristics and beautiful traditions. The survival of Sephardim depends on the strength of Jewish education within this group. Sephardic mores, literature, customs, language, law, and cuisine are directly linked to traditional Jewish sources, which deserve and demand our attention. Can Sephardim continue to exist without a specific educational program to teach them about their rich and noble heritage? The hypothesis of the original doctoral dissertation was that a well-presented curriculum on the current practices of the various Sephardic groups studied will enhance their self-pride and encourage them to enact and preserve their unique Jewish heritage. Without the continuation of the modes and mores of each distinctive Jewish group, the fabric of Jewish life will be weakened and may, God forbid, fulfill the prophecy of Bergman. His only antidote to his foreboding predictions was a fuller Jewish education.[22]

Sephardim can be considered only within the context of Judaism. They cannot be separated from it. Therefore, attendance in a Hebrew day school and in a yeshiva high school is especially important for Sephardic youth.[23] Recent studies have shown the strong correlation between attachment to Judaism and attachment to Sephardic culture.[24] However, even some Sephardim who have had a good Jewish education lack a knowledge of their own Sephardi heritage. They are not aware of their distinctive cultural roots. The reason is because there was no curriculum or book such as this "Teachers Guide to A Treasury of Sephardic Laws and Customs" to assist the teacher in explaining the Sephardic customs for the benefit of all of his students and especially to properly educate his Sephardic students.[25]

Survey of the Literature

A comprehensive search for, and analysis of, written material on the subject of the need for Sephardic laws and customs and how they should be taught in the Jewish schools of America was undertaken by the author. His efforts to secure curricular materials on Sephardic laws and customs from other countries with large Sephardic populations yielded very little information, which reinforced the nature of the problem, for little such material exists elsewhere in the world, including in the State of Israel, where the writer conducted a thorough search of all the major university libraries.

The Alliance Israélite Universelle Schools, with headquarters in Paris, were most cooperative but could not provide an actual curriculum on Sephardic traditional observances. Their files surely contain much material, but the writer received only a publication dated 1903.[26]

The late revered Rabbi Dr. Soleyman Sassoon, of blessed memory, who was then President of Oẓar Hatorah, worldwide, and President of Porat Yosef Yeshiva in Jerusalem, wrote on August 15, 1977, in response to the writer's inquiry for curricular materials on Sephardic laws and customs in the State of Israel,

> I have not been able to find that there are curricula in the schools in which these things are taught. In fact, my impression has been, over the past ten years, that children are intentionally deprived of any knowledge of their background, in order to produce a standard type. Thus, all the beautiful Minhagim tend to be obliterated in this country, unless there are one or two individuals who fight against the stream.[27]

The Director General of Oẓar Hatorah in Iran wrote on October 27, 1977, in reply to an inquiry, that no curriculum exists except an outline for grades one to six, which includes a checklist of terms relating to the Yomin Tovim.[28]

On July 19, 1977, the Director of Oẓar Hatorah in Paris wrote, "Oẓar Hatorah of France is still a young association and we did not yet have the opportunity to publish systematically pedagogic documents for our schools."[29]

The paucity of material and the real need for the development of curricular material on Sephardic laws, customs, history, etc., was brought into excellent focus by the publication of *New Directions: A Publication of the Annual Workshop on Innovative Jewish Education,* jointly sponsored by the American Jewish Committee, Jewish Communal Affairs Department, and the American Association for Jewish Education, entitled "AAJE-AJC Annual Workshop on New Directions in Jewish Education: The Inclusion of a Sephardi Dimension in America Jewish Education," held on March 13, 1978. The *Proceedings* which had just come out, even after the bulk of this study had been written, point out with the greatest of urgency the need for this study and others of a similar nature in other areas of Sephardic interest such as Jewish history, Sephardic heroes, etc.[30]

This writer's educational proposals under the title "Helping Sephardi Students Perpetuate Sephardi Traditions" expressed an impassioned plea for similar type curricular materials to be developed for Sephardic day schools.[31]

Special inspiration for a study of Jewish education under Sephardic auspices in North America can be secured by a careful reading of Haim Zafrani's excellent works describing Jewish education in Arabic lands. His major volume, *Pédagogie Juive en Terre Islam: L'Enseignment Traditionnel de L'Hébreu et du Judaisme au Maroc, Paris,*[32] and some of his pamphlets, describing in great detail the educational system of Morocco, as well as the splendid work of Rabbi David Ovadia, who has written about Jewish education in Sefrou and Fez, Morocco,[33] can give direction to other scholars who wish to further unfold the history of how Jewish life continues (in communities where educational institutions exist).

Despite the apparent lack of any kind of such material about curricula of Halakhah and *minhagim* as taught in North America, it is hoped that the material herein presented will teach Judaism, more so than teach about it.

The writer was among those invited to chair a session at the First International Congress for the Study of the Heritage of Sephardi and Oriental Jewry, held at the Hebrew University in Jerusalem, in June, 1978. Of the more than one hundred papers delivered, only five dealt with topics even remotely related to customs.[34] The emphasis was on history, literature, languages, art culture, folklore, and music.[35] While all these are obviously important components of the Sephardic heritage, they seem to lose all genuine relevance unless a living Sephardic heritage with ongoing observances exists.

Delimitation of the Study

Limitations of Study

The curriculum will be limited to *current* usages of *minhagim* and mores of the four major groups studied. It will not deal with their ancient traditions which have fallen from present-day practice. It will, however, refer to some customs of the "Old Country" which are still followed in varying degrees in North America.

The study will be confined to the various usages of the Syrian, Moroccan, Judeo-Spanish, and Spanish and Portuguese communities, only because their synagogues are among the most widely represented throughout North America. There are also two Iraqi (Bagdadi-style) "Indian" synagogues in Los Angeles and San Francisco. However, much of their *minhagim* has been presented in Dr. Ezekiel N. Musleah's book *On The Banks of the Ganga* and in the works of Abraham ben Yaakob of Hebrew University which are listed in the Bibliography. The customs of the Greek Jews will soon be issued by Dr. Rachel Dalven in *The Jews of Janina,* which she is preparing for publication.[36]

The recent influx of Jews from Afghanistan, Bukhara, and Iran is resulting in the establishment of their own synagogues. These groups will be the subject of the author's next book.[37] There is also one Egyptian synagogue, in Brooklyn, similar in its rituals to traditions of the Syrian community, since many of the Egyptian Jews originated from Syria.[38]

Target Population

This Teacher's Guide will be geared for the upper grades of Sephardic Yeshivot (junior high school grades) or the first three years of Sephardic Yeshiva high schools, as well as for Ashkenazic Yeshiva high schools.

A secondary population who may benefit from this Teacher's

Guide (which was primarily prepared to provide curricular material on Sephardim, for Sephardim to learn more about themselves and the wider spectrum of their own traditions) is the general Ashkenazic Yeshiva high school or Yeshiva junior high school population. Progressive yeshivot, although almost entirely Ashkenazi in their student constituency, should recognize their responsibility to introduce their students to Sephardic *minhagim,* so that their students may attain an overall understanding of Judaism's many-faceted traditions, all of which are equally sacred. The teachers in these schools would adapt *A Treasury of Sephardic Laws and Customs* to their own needs. Some Ashkenazic institutions may wish to offer an elective course on Sephardic laws and customs which would add luster to their regular curriculum. This would be in step with the new and popular American educational vogue to offer more courses about the variegated ethnic cultures. It would surely be an appropriate unit to study under "Israeli Life," since more than 60 percent of Israel's population are Sephardim.[39]

Other adaptations by a teacher, such as for afternoon Hebrew high schools or adult education programs, could be easily accomplished. The book *A Treasury of Sephardic Laws and Customs* was carefully prepared, with an extensive translation of the Hebrew terminology, a Glossary, and an Index, with the thought in mind that the text could be used by even those teachers who do not have an extensive background in Halakhah. These are simply bonus alternative usages for the material, which is essentially geared to a two-year cycle in a Yeshiva junior high (with omission of the third cycle) or a three-year cycle for yeshiva high school.

Curricular Organization

The following is a suggested curriculum plan. In this Teacher's Guide the teacher will find four model lessons which will demonstrate how this material can be integrated into an overall classroom lesson on the topics which are treated specifically from the perspective of showing distinctive Sephardic ritual usages. However, teaching methodology per se is beyond the purview of this work.

The curricular material on *A Treasury of Sephardic Laws and Customs,* as reflected among the four Sephardic communities, will be presented to the students on the "Spiral Unfoldment Method."[40] Although much of this material on customs will have already been presented during the first five years of Yeshiva education in the curriculum in a more elementary fashion, this subject matter should now serve both as a review of the old material and as an opportunity to add higher dimensions of understanding relative to the material. Simpler and more universal conceptual material is presented for the younger students at the lower grades of the junior high school. As the material becomes more complex and sophisticated, it is accordingly offered to the more advanced grades. The discretion of the teacher and principal should determine which material should be taught (or omitted) in the third cycle for the third year of high school.

Significance for Education

Few would disagree that the current absence of a course of study of the major Sephardic groups who reside in North America, and the resultant lessening of religious observance, is a natural outgrowth of the neglect in the Sephardic community due to the lack of self-knowledge of their traditions. It is contended that a rich and enriching curriculum on *A Treasury of Sephardic Laws and Customs* will further strengthen or restore the proud identification with their distinctive heritage which was always characteristic of Sephardic Jewry. In contrast to those Sephardic communities who are spiritually impoverished, in the sense of ritual observance by the masses, the Syrian community has several Yeshivot and can now boast of many rabbis and young Talmudic scholars who have attended Yeshivot.[41] These are the young men and women who are successfully perpetuating their heritage by living full Jewish lives for themselves and by conducting seminars and Shabbatons to inspire other Syrian youth to do likewise.[42] That measure of success is here today because, as far back as 1917, the Syrian Talmud Torah, then under the guidance of Hakham Mayer Waknin, consisted of one hundred twenty students who attended religious studies for three hours on Sunday, four hours daily during the week (except Friday), and five hours on Saturday afternoon. That curriculum provided a total of twenty-four hours a week of intensive Jewish education which is more than the time devoted to Torah studies in many of our modern Yeshivot today.[43] It was there, under such tutelage, and under the leadership of Rev. Joseph A. Benyunes, that the heritage of the Syrian community was preserved and passed on to the younger generation. This was accomplished amidst all the turmoil of the immigrant families struggling to accommodate themselves to a new, wonderful, and strange land. Whereas it is true that they did not have a written curriculum on their own customs and traditions, and certainly nothing in a formal syllabus about other Sephardic customs, they did succeed in breeding a new generation of regular worshippers and staunch observers in the Syrian or Eastern Sephardic heritage. This was done by the rabbis and teachers who instructed them, by their word, and their own fine example.[44]

It would, therefore, appear that in a community which encourages its youth to secure Jewish day school education on the elementary and high school levels, and perhaps even on the college level, there is hope for the survival of a living heritage for many generations to come. Our task, therefore, is to provide Sephardic students who attend Sephardic day schools with a rich cultural offering reflecting their own respective heritage in its many varieties. This will encourage a greater pride of identification with the traditions of their fathers, and may enable them to prevail, despite their small numbers. This Teacher's Guide will also enable the instructor to teach about the customs of other Sephardic groups who abound in North America, for example, Syrians, Moroccans, Judeo-Spanish, and Spanish and Portuguese, who, for the most part, are unfamiliar with each other's customs.

If, as we said earlier, it is difficult to conceive a Sephardism separated from Judaism, it is impossible to perceive Judaism without its Sephardic component! How could Judaism have survived without the contributions of Maimonides, Alfasi, Abravanel, and Joseph Caro, just to mention a few of the Sephardic luminaries whose monumental contributions to Jewish scholarship form the core of any meaningful Yeshiva curriculum today. It is, therefore, essential that we recall our debt to the past by bringing to light the continuing religious and cultural heritage of Sephardim. We must unveil for the Sephardim, Ashkenazim, and the Jewish world at large, many of the enduring contributions which have been made in many lands by Sephardic scholars during the past four or five centuries. The author is therefore pleased that he has been assured by leading educators in the Sephardic Yeshivot, and in some Ashkenazic Yeshivot as well, that this Teacher's Guide to *A Treasury of Sephardic Laws and Customs* will answer a basic need and will be used in the schools where the book will be used as a textbook.

Relatedness to Jewish Education

The deplorable status of curricular materials in the field of Sephardic laws and customs even in those parts of the world which have much larger Sephardic populations than America should emphasize, in bold relief, the critical need for these Jewish educational materials worldwide and particularly in North America. Here, it is especially important for the minority Sephardic community (who in North America are not a majority of the Jewish population, as the Sephardim are in Israel) to be morally and spiritually bolstered and inspired by the wealth of sources on their background and tradition. Similarly, the new generation of American Sephardim and American Ashkenazim, who are together the major supporters of the State of Israel, must be exposed to the multifaceted beauty of Sephardic customs and must come to respect these as part of the totality of the Jewish religious experience. The concept that the Sephardim represent exotic, archaic, backward, and strange mores, not intrinsic to Jewish teachings, must be dispelled. In fact, in some cases, the distinctive Sephardic *minhag* more closely conforms to Halakhah than the Ashkenazi observance.[45] There is almost always a basis for Sephardic *minhag* in Halakhah. It was recognized long ago that in Judaism there is more than one acceptable practice: "Both are the words of the Living God" is a guiding principle in Jewish life.[46] Mutual understanding among all

Jews, as *Klal Yisrael*, with one God, and one Torah, can only come about through an education which will present the totality of Jewish life and customs, which by definition must include the mores of Sephardim. A knowledge and understanding of Sephardic customs, which are now beginning to be brought into focus in America and which are so readily apparent to the American tourist in Israel, is imperative.[47] In fact, the security of the State of Israel may more closely hinge on that kind of mutual understanding and respect among its population than the external problem of the Arab enemy.[48] It is hoped that this study will reinforce that kind of understanding and mutual respect and high regard among all Jews.

Therefore, *A Treasury of Sephardic Laws and Customs* should be regarded as a unique contribution to the field of Jewish education in North America. It should also serve as a meaningful educational instrument for England, Australia, South Africa, and other large English-speaking Sephardic and Ashkenazic communities. It could serve as a model and inspiration for the development of similar materials in France and other countries where large numbers of Sephardim and Ashkenazim dwell and conduct Jewish day schools.

One last word about the importance of this work as relates to the Sephardim themselves. We can note from the general deterioration of religious life (which affects Ashkenazim and Sephardim alike) that, among Sephardim in the State of Israel and in the Diaspora, *when they do* adhere to religion, it is generally according to the heritage of their fathers.[49] The adherence to tradition handed down from one generation to the other is the most significant explanation for the ability of the Sephardim to have survived until this time. It is not a rare phenomenon to note that in some communities Sephardic Jews have almost neglected Judaism rather than succumb to the adoption of Ashkenazic laws and customs, or to become part of the religious establishment of Ashkenazic Jewry. It was therefore an added impetus to develop this particular work on Sephardic customs and to develop a comprehensive curriculum on their own traditions, for their own institutions, and for their own use, which could prove to be a vital instrument in preserving these segments of the Sephardic community for Judaism at large.

Special mention should also be made in reference to the excellent introduction to *Yalkut Haminhagim,* which describes "Al Haminhag" (About Custom) by Y. Goldschmidt. He beautifully describes how the true spirit of the enriching and inspiring Jewish experience of observing our holy days or our special occasions is enhanced by the customs enacted by the different communities. Using the Shabbat as an example, he demonstrates how our observance goes far beyond mere cessation from working, but involves our treating the occasion in a special way by dressing for the Sabbath, preparing special foods, praying the various worship services, conducting the home observances, studying the Torah, using the day to support and strengthen social and family relationships, etc.[50] As educators, it is our special goal to motivate our students to love the *mizvot* and to perform them in a manner which will sustain their commitment to the preservation of our distinctive and noble heritage. The *minhagim* will more effectively retain, strengthen, and inspire this kind of attachment to the past, involvement in the present-day Jewish experience, and secure the survival of our unique and time-hallowed mores and values than most other subjects we teach.

Pronunciation of Hebrew

The Ashkenazic and Sephardic pronunciations of Hebrew have, for a long time, been the subject of much scientific research and were often dealt with by the rabbis in the various times and places in their responsa, especially in connection with the question of proper pronunciation of the liturgy.

The teacher should familiarize himself with the various theories on this fascinating subject as is referred to in the comprehensive work by H.J. Zimmels entitled *Ashkenazim and Sephardim: Their Relations, Differences, and Problems as Reflected in the Rabbinical Responsa,* published by Oxford University Press, London, 1958. Briefly stated, Zimmels categorizes the three prevalent theories as follows: (1) The Sephardic pronunciation is the original, while the Ashkenazic pronunciation developed in later times under the influence of the environment. (2) Both pronunciations date from antiquity, being a continuation of the two different pronunciations in use in Palestine and Babylonia, like Syriac, which has been handed down to us in twofold pronunciation. (3) Ashkenazic pronunciation originated in Palestine, while the Sephardic pronunciation was produced by the Jews in Spain. The second theory seems to be the favorite among scholars nowadays.[51]

This matter requires much extensive study, and it is not our purpose to delve into the matter in any great depth.

An article by Prof. Herman P. Salomon, editor of *The American Sephardi*, entitled "Hebrew Pronunciation Among Western Sephardim" (*American Sephardi*, vol. I, no. 2 [Sivan 5727/June 1967], published by the Sephardic Studies Program of Yeshiva University), presents an interesting study on the pronunciation practices of the Spanish and Portuguese Jews.[52]

For purposes of this study, the Transliteration Rules of the *Encyclopaedia Judaica* (Keter Publishing House, Jerusalem, 1972), as presented in its Index Volume on page 90, which designates Hebrew and Semitic languages, have been followed, using the "General" rather than the "Scientific" format.[53]

It is hoped that the extra effort taken to preserve the authentic pronunciation by the respective groups will facilitate the efforts of the teacher to properly render the word in the Hebrew in general accordance with the accepted pronunciation of the respective groups.

Whereas we note that there are other differences which are effective, it was not possible (nor deemed necessary in a study of this nature) to make any further distinctions between the various Sephardic forms of pronunciations. These are left to the discretion and skill of the individual teacher to communicate in his respective community.

Suggested Cycles for Teaching Different Grades

the material in

A Treasury of Sephardic Laws and Customs

The following is a Three-Cycle design for the curriculum on teaching *A Treasury of Sephardic Laws and Customs*. It may be used accordingly by the junior high schools and high schools in either of the following manners.

Junior high schools which do not have a specific high school into which their students flow for a continued curriculum may wish to incorporate the materials designed for the first two Cycles in Grades 7 and 8. The subject matter of the third Cycle, which is of a more sophisticated level, should be completely omitted. Hopefully they will learn this material later.

For junior high schools which do feed into a specific high school system with whom they coordinate curriculum, the teacher may wish to divide the material in Cycle I over a two-year period, covering half during Grade 7 and half during Grade 8. Cycles II and III would then be covered in the Yeshiva high school in Grades 9, 10, and 11, respectively, or in Grades 9 and 10 (a full year's Cycle each grade) depending upon the specific needs of the students and the time available.

For Yeshiva high schools which do not coordinate with a Yeshiva junior high school, for whom this will be a self-contained curriculum, the three Cycles would be covered in Grades 9, 10, and 11. A major consideration in limiting the Cycles to three, rather than four, grades is because nowadays in many high schools the fourth year is uncertain, either because of students entering early admissions college programs, co-op programs, or "Study in Israel" programs. Thus, by covering the material in a three-year period the maximum number of students will be exposed to the study of this special body of Jewish knowledge.

The specific goal in the preparation of this sacred subject matter is to provide the teacher with the necessary background for each of the four groups of Sephardim treated. The students will come to a greater appreciation of the four major groups of Sephardic Jews who exist as living, dynamic subgroups of the total Sephardic and general Jewish communities in North America. Each of these four groups expresses its living heritage in synagogues found throughout the continent.

It is, of course, expected that the teacher will also refer to the abundant resources which depict the usages of the Ashkenazim so that the Sephardic student will have an understanding of his Ashkenazi brother's customs as well. Since the Jewish educational curriculum materials are predominantly, if not almost totally, based upon the Ashkenazi customs, this study does not deal with that subject matter.[54]

For the Ashkenazi students in the junior high school or high school of our Yeshivot, the study of these customs and traditions will serve to broaden their understanding of the rich and distinctive observances of their Sephardi coreligionists in North America. Since many of these same Ashkenazi students will hopefully visit or study in the State of Israel, this body of knowledge will serve as a major resource of background information to help them achieve a better understanding of religious life in Israel.

In order to facilitate the teaching of the subject matter, the special material relating to each chapter of *A Treasury of Sephardic Laws and Customs* provides the teacher with the following important material:

1. A Basic Sources reading list for the student (and teacher) to get an overview of the subject matter from authentic Sephardic sources.
2. Questions for Review or Homework.
3. Topics for Discussion in Class. Most topics were selected because they represent some problem or controversy in Halakhah.
4. In addition, the extensive Bibliography in *A Treasury of Sephardic Laws and Customs* lists all of the sources quoted or reviewed by the writer. The sources will also serve the teacher who may wish to delve into any of the areas covered in greater detail with a carefully screened selection of appropriate books and studies on the topics. Most of these books may be found in the Sephardic Reference Room of the Mendel Gottesman Library of Yeshiva University in New York City.

As mentioned earlier, methodology of teaching Jewish laws and customs is beyond the purview of this study. It is expected that the professional teacher will have been trained in the formulation of appropriate teaching strategies and methodology, whether it be for Ashkenazic customs, Sephardic customs, or other such subject matter. Nevertheless a word of caution is in order. Only for a class with an in-depth understanding of classical Torah sources should the mystical or Kabbalistic reasons for many of the customs be emphasized, lest they appear as mere superstition. To the scholar acquainted with the richness of the Sephardic contributions to the development of mystical teaching, these reasons are a source of enlightenment. However, to the untutored, the mystical literature may provide a distorted view which could mistakenly appear to be primitive, which is not at all the case. The sensitive teacher should therefore handle these aspects with special care and reverence.

An explanation in regard to the customs of Moroccan Jewry in particular will be helpful. It will be found that the bulk of the references are to practices of communities in Morocco rather than to communities in North America, per se. The reason is that the new Moroccan community is still a community in transition. They still continuously arrive from Morocco, France, and Israel. Their traditions are therefore presently being transplanted into the various congregations in North America with which they identify. Therefore, until an amalgam of these communities takes place over the next decade, the authentic traditions of the "Old Country" seem to prevail as the current usage, for the most part. Therefore the old is still the new, and the Moroccan heritage is being preserved in North America to the fullest possible extent.

The pages following the notes to the Introduction present an outline of the suggested Cycles to be followed by the junior high school and high school teachers.

Notes to Introduction

1. *Talmud Babli,* 20 vols. (New York: Yam Hatalmud Shulsinger Bros., Linotyping, 1948) *Erubin* 13b.

2. H.J. Zimmels, *Ashkenazim and Sephardim* (London: Oxford University Press, 1958), p. 147.

3. Richard D. Barnett, *The Sephardi Heritage,* 2 vols. (London: Valentine Mitchell and Co., 1971), p. 5.

4. Abraham Ben Yaacob, ed., *Yalkut Minhagim* (Jerusalem: Misrad Haḥinukh Vehatarbut Agaf Haḥinukh Hadati, 1969), pp. 8–9.

5. Marc D. Angel, "The Sephardim of the United States: An Exploration Study," *American Jewish Year Book,* 1973, p. 80.

6. Barnett, *Sephardi Heritage,* p. 1.

7. Victor D. Sanua, "Contemporary Studies on Sephardi Jews in the United States" (Paper presented at the Sixth World Congress of Studies, Jerusalem, August, 1973), mimeographed, p. 1. See also Liliane Levy Winn, "President's Message," *Sephardi World,* 3, no. 1 (September 1977): 3. Although Sanua quotes 150,000-200,000, since his study the immigration of Sephardim to America has increased.

8. Sanua, "Contemporary Studies," pp. 6–7. See also Angel, "Sephardim of the United States," p. 116.

9. Angel, "Sephardim of the United States," p. 88.

10. Elihu Bergman, "The American Jewish Population Erosion," *Midstream* 23, no. 8 (October 1977): 10. See also "The American Jew Today," *Newsweek,* March 1, 1971, p. 61.

11. Sanua, "Contemporary Studies," p. 11.

12. Ibid, pp. 8–9. Also see Jean Claude Lasry, "Jewish Intermarriage in Montreal, 1962–1972," *Jewish Social Studies,* 37 (1975): 267–278, where he describes exogamy for North African Jewish males at 61 percent and for females at 32 percent making for an average of 50 percent.

13. Hayyim Cohen, "Sephardi Jews in the United States: Marriage with Ashkenazim and Non-Jews," *Dispersion and Unity* (Jerusalem: Hebrew University, 1971–72), p. 154.

14. Sanua, "Contemporary Studies," p. 5.

15. *American Sephardi Federation,* "Report of Activities" (mimeographed), August 1–September 14, 1977, p. 2.

16. Angel, "Sephardim of the United States," p. 106.

17. H.J. Campeas, "Sephardic Studies Program," *American Sephardi* 1, no. 1 (December 1966): 4.

18. Angel, "Sephardim of the United States," p. 110.

19. Joseph A.D. Sutton, *Magic Carpet: Aleppo In Flatbush* (New York: Thayer-Jacoby, 1979), p. 96. See also Angel, "Sephardim of the United States", p. 110.

20. Angel, "Sephardim of the United States," p. 126.

21. Ibid.

22. Bergman, "Population Erosion," pp. 13–14.

23. Angel, "Sephardim of the United States," p. 136.

24. Sanua, "Contemporary Studies," p. 5.

25. "Proceedings," *New Directions: A Publication of Annual Workshop on Innovative Jewish Education* (Arthur Brody's presentation for the Conference on Innovative Projects in Jewish Education), (New York: March 13, 1978), p. 6.

26. *Alliance Israélite Universelle: Instructions Générales Pour les Professeurs* (Paris: Seige de la Societe, 1903), pp. 1–109. This outdated book discusses religious Jewish education on pp. 16, 26, 29, and 30–37, which constitutes the complete outline for religious education in the Alliance Israélite Universelle schools. Also a letter from Eugene Weill, Secretary General, Alliance Israélite Universelle Paris, July 6, 1977, to The Haham Dr. Solomon Gaon, Chief Rabbi of the Sephardic Congregations of the British Commonwealth, indicates that the Alliance would make an effort to uncover more material, but only the above-cited material was sent.

27. Letter from Rabbi Dr. Soleyman D. Sassoon, President of Oẓar Hatorah and President of Porat Yosef Yeshiva, Jerusalem, August, 15, 1977.

28. Letter from Rabbi Joseph L. Schuchatowitz, Director-General, Oẓar Hatorah–Iran, Teheran, October 27, 1977.

29. Letter from J. Charbit, Director of Oẓar Hatorah, Paris, July 18, 1977.

30."Proceedings," Presentation by Mr. Yehudah Rosenman, Director, Jewish Communal Affairs Department, American Committee, p. 1.

31. Ibid, Presentation by Rabbi Herbert C. Dobrinsky, Executive Assistant to the President, Yeshiva University, pp. 57–66.

32. Haim Zafrani, *Pédagogie Juive en Terre D'Islam, L'Enseignement Traditionnel de l'Hébreu et du Judaisme au Maroc* (Paris: Librairie D'Amerique et D'Orient, Adrien Maissonneuve, 1969).

33. David Ovadia, *Kehillat Sefrou, Morocco: The Community of Sefrou, Morocco,* 3 vols. (Jerusalem: By the Author, 1975).

34. Shlomo Kidron, ed., "Papers to be Delivered at the First International Congress for the Study of the Heritage of Sephardi and Oriental Jewry," *Jewish Cultural News,* 2, no. 1 (Jerusalem: Electrolene Typesetters for the Cultural Department of the World Jewish Congress, June 1978), pp. 5–6.

35. Ibid.

36. Rachel Dalven, Professor Emeritus of Ladycliff College, Highland Falls, is editor of *The Sephardic Scholar* and has published books and articles in the fields of English and Greek literature and theater as well as on the Jews of Greece.

37. As was anticipated, new synagogues were established by Iranian Jews in Forest Hills, New York; Los Angeles, California; and elsewhere.

38. Congregation Ahaba V'Ahava, located on Ocean Parkway in Brooklyn, New York, recently received attention in the newspapers following the reestablishment of political relations between Egypt and the State of Israel.

39. Nessim Gaon, "The Sephardi Presence in Israel," *Sephardi World* (New York: American Sephardi Federation), April, 1979, p. 4.

40. Under this educational approach, simpler material is presented to the younger children, and the subject matter progresses in its complexity and sophistication, as it is used for each successive class.

41. Sanua, "Contemporary Studies," p. 5.

42. The Sephardic Community Activities Program of Yeshiva University conducts Torah leadership Seminars for Sephardic youth in the Greater New York area and other parts of the country under the leadership of Rabbi M. Mitchell Serels, Director of Sephardic Community Activities at Yeshiva University. These activities have been held since 1966. In addition, the American Sephardi Federation Youth Movement conducts similar projects on a national scale and has held three such youth conventions. The Yeshiva University effort includes outreach programs to Latin American countries under the title of "Realidad."

43. Sutton, *Magic Carpet,* pp. 24–26.

44. Ibid, p. 25.

45. Zimmels, *Ashkenazim and Sephardim,* pp. 205–232.

46. Talmud, *Erubin* 13b.

47. "Proceedings," *New Directions* (see above no. 25). "One whole segment of our cultural heritage, the Sephardi dimension has been absent from the Jewish school curriculum. And I can speak very personally; I know very little about Sephardi history, culture and tradition. I come from nine/ten years of congregational schooling—

and none of it was taught us. I go to Israel and I feel even a bigger ignoramus because I see a vast Sephardi reality in Israel society." p. 6.

48. Z. Frank, "Israel's 'Black Panthers'—Two Perspectives," *American Zionist* 62, no. 1 (September 1971): 32–35.

49. Angel, "Sephardim of the United States," pp. 91–92.

50. Ben Yaacob, *Yalkut*, pp. 7–8

51. Zimmels, *Ashkenazim and Sephardim*, pp. 82–83.

52. Herman P. Salomon, "Hebrew Pronunciation Among Western Sephardim," *American Sephardi* 1, no. 1 (June 1967): 20.

53. Cecil Roth, ed., *Encyclopaedia Judaica* (Jerusalem: Keter Publishing, 1972), 1:90.

54. Two appropriate English publications on Ashkenazic customs which could be used by the teacher are: Abraham Chill's *The Minhagim, The Customs and Ceremonies of Judaism: Their Origins and Rationale* (New York: Sepher Hermon Press, 1979), and Hayim Halevy Donin's *To Be a Jew* (New York: Basic Books, 1972).

CYCLE I

The Daily Way of Life

Respect for parents, elders, teachers	Chapter 8
Acts of Kindness	Chapter 8
Laws of Charity	Chapter 9

Special Family Occasions — Chapter 2

Bar Miẓvah	
Cantillation of Torah and Prophets (for *Bar Miẓvah* preparation)	See Bibliography
Laws of Reading the Torah (for *Bar Miẓvah* preparation)	Chapter 10

Signs of the Covenant — Chapter 6

Tefillin
Ẓiẓit and *Tallit*
Mezuzah

Shabbat — Chapter 11

Preparing for Shabbat
The Friday Evening Ritual
Shabbat Morning Services and *Kiddush*
Shabbat Lunch and Afternoon Services
Moẓaei Shabbat Observances

The Festivals — Part IV (See appropriate chapters)

1. A review of the customs relating to each Festival following the calendar cycle according to one's own usage. Each year a comparison of *one* of the *other groups* should add a new dimension of understanding to the Festivals as lived and expressed by other Jews. In the third cycle, the study of *two* other groups should be undertaken, as it is presumed that one will, by that time, be adequately trained in his own *minhagim*.

2. The Laws of Rosh Ḥodesh — Chapter 15
The Laws of the Month of Elul — Chapter 16

Daily Worship

Shaḥarit, Minḥa, Arbit, as discussed and prayed in the school setting.

CYCLE II

The Daily Way of Life — Chapter 9

A survey of the institutions which perpetuate the principles of Jewish concern for the welfare of our brethren:
Gemilat Ḥesed Loan Funds
Bikur Ḥolim Societies or Committees
Ḥebra Kaddisha
Homes for the Aged and Infirm
Welfare Funds to Care for Local Needy

The Dietary Laws — Chapter 7

Forbidden Foods
Requirements of *Sheḥita*
"Kashering" of Meat Through *Meliḥa,* Broiling, etc.
Forbidden Mixtures of Foods, etc.
Making Unfit Vessels *Kasher*
Immersion of Vessels
Ḥallah

Special Family Occasions — Chapter 1

Birth and Naming of Children
Berit Milah
Zebed Habat
Pidyon Haben
Laws of Burial, Mourning, Comforting Mourners, *Kaddish, Hashkabot* and Annual Memorials. Omit *Reḥiẓat Hamet* ("Washing of the Dead" in second cycle) — Chapter 5

The Synagogue — Chapter 10

The responsibilities of a synagogue to the community

The responsibilities of the individual to the synagogue
Personal conduct in synagogue
The Writing of a *Sefer Torah*
The Priestly Benedictions
Special Prayers
Shema Yisrael
Blessings Over the Torah
Blessings for Various Occasions
Synagogues—religious appurtenances, personnel, officers, etc.

The Sabbath Chapter 11

A review of observances of the specific group's customs and those of one other group. Detailed study of forbidden "works" on Sabbath, matters forbidden by the Torah, by the Rabbis, etc.

The Festivals Part IV (See appropriate chapters)

Review of our Festivals plus the study of one other group's Festivals according to calendar cycle.
Special study of the Fast-Days: Fast of Gedalia, 10th of Tebet; Fast of Esther; 17th of Tammuz; Tisha BeAb; Private Fast-Days.

CYCLE III

The Daily Way of Life Chapter 9

The pursuit of Justice: the role of the *Bet Din* in modern Jewish life

The Dietary Laws Chapter 12

Detailed laws relating to observance of Pesaḥ

Signs of the Covenant Chapter 10

Comparative study of all types of *Tefillin*

Special Family Occasions Chapter 8

The education of children

Marriage
Relationship of Husband-Wife
(Taharat Hamishpaḥa)
Modesty
Divorce — Chapter 4. See also Appendix A
Ḥaliẓah — Chapter 4. See also Appendix A
Taharat hamet—"Washing of the Dead" — Chapter 5
See also Appendix A

The Synagogue

Comparison of prayer books in daily worship services of the four groups:
Shaḥarit, Minḥa, Arbit — Chapter 10

The Sabbath — Chapter 11

Study of customs of two other groups

Festivals — Part IV (See appropriate chapters)

Study of the observances of two groups
The second day of a Festival of the Diaspora
Laws relating to this observance when visiting Israel and vice versa, etc.
Details of *Teshubah* for High Holy Days
Details on construction of a *Sukkah* and appropriate laws of walls, *Sekhakh*, etc.
Details of *Shetar Mekhirah* for Pesaḥ
Study of *Azharot* for Shabuot
Careful study of Tishah BeAb Fast laws and prayers

Laws Relating to Ereẓ Yisrael — Chapter 9

Responsibility for Israel's survival
Aliyah—Yishuv Ereẓ Yisrael

MODEL LESSON 1

CYCLE I

TEFILLIN

(Reenactment of a classroom session)

Target Population

Class of twelve-year-old boys in Yeshiva junior high school. They have been studying laws of *tefillin* in preparation for their putting on *tefillin* and their Bar Miẓvah.

Time

A class period of fifty minutes.

INTRODUCTION

The teacher had given the students advance assignments to study the following basic sources (assigning different sections to various students in the class): *Shulḥan Arukh, Oraḥ Ḥayyim* 25–37; *Kaf Haḥayyim* (same chapters as listed in *Shulḥan Arukh*); *Mekor Ḥayyim Hashalem,* Volume 1, 29–36; *Kiẓur Shulḥan Arukh Hashalem,* Vol. 1, 10; *Ben Ish Ḥay* "Parashiot Vayera" and "Ḥayyei Sarah"; *Yalkut Meam Loez,* Shemot Gimmel: 1023–1026; Debarim Bet: 554–558; 563–564; He asked them to prepare brief oral reports for the next session.

In previous sessions the teacher had covered a discussion about the order of the biblical portions placed in the *tefillin.* He discussed how the *tefillin* are made, and the differences between the order of the *parashiot* as understood by Rashi and by Rabbenu Tam. He had discussed the various laws relating to the appearance, construction, and detailed description of the *parashiot* as described in the Mishna *Menaḥot* 3, 7, and many of the halahkic matters discussed in the Talmud *Menaḥot,* folios 34b, 35b, 44a, 36a, and 36b.

Students were given guide sheets to help them achieve the following goals. They also received drawings which show the different Sephardic ways of wearing *tefillin* as well as the Ashkenazic way.

OBJECTIVES OF THE LESSON WERE:

Informational

1. To give specific knowledge on the Sephardic tradition for putting on *tefillin* as regards:
   A. The blessing(s) for the *tefillin.*
   B. The manner in which the *tefillin* are placed on the hand, head, palm, and fingers.
   C. The position that one is in, either sitting or standing, when reciting the blessing(s) and putting on the *tefillin.*

Skills

A. The manner of putting on and removing *tefillin.*
B. Orientation on the inspection of *tefillin.*

Values

A. To understand how one conducts himself if he accidentally drops his *tefillin* (fasting or *pidyon taanit* [charity]).
B. To learn when *tefillin* are worn and when they are not worn by Sephardim (such as at time of special *teshuba* and when one can have a constant awareness of *kedusha*).
C. Some of the general reasons why we perform the commandments of *tefillin* as described above (symbolic of service of God in thought *[shel rosh]* and deed *[shel yad]*).

MATERIALS

1. Three pairs of *tefillin* were present. There was also an old pair of *tefillin* which was open so that the *parashiot* inside could

be seen by the students. Photographs of how the *tefillin* are placed on the heads and hands, both Ashkenazic and the two different Sephardic styles, were again provided for the students with the use of an overhead projector.

Of the three pairs of *tefillin*, one pair was *Rashi tefillin*, one was Rabbenu Tam *tefillin*, and the third pair was the much larger Ashkenazic Ḥassidic *tefillin*.

2. The class was given a new guide sheet relating to the different styles of putting on *tefillin* with basic questions to denote the differences.

METHOD

The teacher conducted a brief discussion with the students to review the sources from the Bible, Talmud, and *Shulḥan Arukh* on some of the previous laws which had been covered in earlier lessons. Some students delivered brief reports.

The teacher asked questions of the students to determine their level of prior knowledge about the age at which a young man should begin to put on *tefillin* in order to prepare for Bar Miẓvah, etc.

The importance of the Bar Miẓvah was stressed, since all the members in this all male class would be celebrating their Bar Miẓvah during the course of the year. Thus, this kind of discussion served as a major motivational factor in the lesson.

Also the first occasion to formally mark the initial putting on of *tefillin* by the lad was spoken of for motivational purposes.

All of the information described in the guide sheet for the homework was reviewed by questions or reports by students lasting from 2 to 5 minutes.

The teacher invited volunteers to demonstrate the various customs of putting on *tefillin* within the Sephardic community and within the Ashkenazic community as well. Students were encouraged to note the differences. They noted the differences on the guide sheet which the teacher had provided for this purpose.

PRESENTATION (rendered in the present tense to give full flavor of the interaction)

Teacher: How do we fulfill the *mizvah* of *hanaḥat tefillin* according to our individual traditions, and why do we do so?

Student: This refers to the putting on of the *tefillin shel yad* and the *tefillin shel rosh,* in fulfillment of the biblical quotations we have already reviewed.

Teacher: Which do we put on first and why?

Student: Since it says in the Bible "And you shall tie them *le-ot,* as a sign, upon your hand and they shall be as frontlets between thine eyes," we put them on the hand first and then on the head.

(The teacher has a student stand in front of the class to demonstrate the various stages of how the *tefillin* are put on when the discussion takes place. At each stage the student enacts the topic under discussion. First he puts on *tefillin* on the arm *while sitting,* recites the *berakha, then rises,* puts the *tefillin* on his hand, then finishes winding the first *tefillin* around the hand and fingers, etc.)

Teacher: When and how many blessings do Sephardim make when putting on the *tefillin*?

Student: The *one* blessing which we normally make is *Lehaniaḥ tefillin* (which will suffice *unless we are interrupted,* in which case we will have to say a second blessing over the *tefillin* on the head, *Al mizvat tefillin*) and we make the blessing just as we are about to tighten the strap around the upper muscle of our left hand opposite the heart.

(The teacher discusses the whole question of blessings usually being recited *before* the performance of the *mizvot,* using examples of how we make the blessings before: being called to the Torah; reading the *Megillah;* putting on the *tallit;* lighting Ḥanukkah candles; etc. All of these show that the blessing is recited *beforehand.* The distinction can be made between them based upon the talmudic discussion of all these other *mizvot* and how the *tefillin* are blessed upon as we have indeed already put on the strap but just *before* we tighten it into place.

The teacher calls for additional volunteers to show different ways of how Sephardim put on *tefillin.* (Students volunteer.)

Teacher: What position are we in when we put on the *tefillin* on the hand?

Student: We *sit* for putting on the *shel yad* and recite the *berakha* in that position, and we *stand* for putting on the *shel rosh,* which is normally without a *berakha* unless we were *mafsik* (interrupted) in which case we would recite the second blessing, *Al miẓvat tefillin,* while standing. We also *stand* for tying the straps around the hand and around the fingers.

Teacher: Can anyone tell us *why* we change our positions in the manner that has been described?

(Some students offer answers but none are correct.)

Teacher: The *Shela* instructs us from the talmudic tractate *Ḥullin* 112b that this is our custom, since it is all *one miẓvah* being performed in several parts. We begin by putting the *tefillin* on our left hand, which is normally the weaker hand, and tie the *tefillin* from the inside to the outside (which is different than the Ashkenazic method) and then rise to do the second portion of the *miẓvah* by putting the *tefillin* on our head and adjusting the knot in the back of the nape of the neck properly. We remain standing while we tie the portion around the hand and the special way we tie it around the finger because we are reciting *V'erastikh* ("and I will betroth myself unto thee..."), which is symbolic of our marriage to God. Therefore we must be standing, just as the groom stands when he places the ring on the finger of his bride.

How many pairs of *tefillin* do we put on?

Student: Those people who want to fulfill the commandment according to all of the various versions offered by Rashi and Rabbenu Tam put on two pairs of *tefillin.*

Teacher: When do they do this?

Student: I have seen the Syrian Chief Rabbi put both pairs of *tefillin* on at the same time, that is, two pairs of *tefillin* (one *Rashi tefillin* and one *Rabbenu Tam tefillin*) on his arm and two pairs of *tefillin* on his head in the same fashion. He wears them together throughout the service. Can I show you how he does it?

Teacher: Yes, please do. I am surprised you know how, since that is truly rare in this country.

(The student begins to put on two pairs of *tefillin*.)

Teacher: The fact is that it was the custom of many of our Sephardim in Syria, Morocco, and other countries to do so, and many still do so in the Land of Israel. Class! What does that custom explain that should be self-evident from these holy items (referring to the *tefillin*) I have on my desk?

(No one answers.)

Now you can see it is clear why the Sephardic *tefillin* had to be made much smaller if both pairs were to be worn at the same time!

(Volunteer student who had gone to corner to put on the *tefillin*, turns around to face class while wearing both pairs of *tefillin*.)

Teacher: Tell us, if all Sephardim do this, how come we don't see it more frequently here in America?

Student: That's because most who put on two pairs of *tefillin* put on the *Rashi tefillin* first, remove them after the *Amidah*, and then put on the *Rabbenu Tam tefillin*. I also read that those who wore both *tefillin* normally were considered to be the *talmidei ḥakhamim*, the more pious members of the community. They would mock a layman who did this if he was not extremely pious in all matters!

Teacher: Well spoken, you are absolutely correct! Now, what happens if someone drops his *tefillin*?

Student: I read that *you have to fast* as a sign of asking forgiveness for being negligent while performing a holy *miẓvah*, is that right?

Teacher: Usually, one is asked to fast, but if for some reason he is unable to do so, he is asked to make a contribution to *ẓedakah* as *pidyon taanit* (in redemption of fasting). Tell me: Would you have to fast twice if you dropped both *tefillin*?

Student: I don't think so, but I will look up that point if you want me to!

Teacher: Yes, please do look it up and give us the answer at our next session. Now let us determine at what point in the service we put on *tefillin*. Who knows the answer?

Student: Usually at *Lamenaẓẓeaḥ binginot mizmor shir*, which is immediately before *Barukh sheamar*, although some put them on right after *Birkot hashaḥar.*

(The teacher asks a few more questions based on the guide sheet for the homework assignment and then says:)

Teacher: Well, it is gratifying to see that you people have taken your assignments seriously and you sure are familiar with the Halakhah, which makes me very proud. *Ḥazak ubarukh!* But tell me something else. At which services do all Sephardim put on *tefillin,* and when don't they put on *tefillin,* which may be different from the practices of some other groups? Who can report on this? I would like a very comprehensive answer!

Student: Sephardim put on *tefillin* at the afternoon *Minha* service of all fast-days. Most Sephardim don't put them on, on Tisha BeAb in the morning (although there are some whose custom it is to put them on Tisha BeAb morning at home privately, and then they come to synagogue without wearing their *tefillin*). Also, Sephardim never put on *tefillin* on Ḥol Hamoed, which, just like Shabbat, is considered to be a "sign" (*ot*), and since the purpose of *tefillin* is to be a sign, there is no need for a double sign. Syrians observe putting on *tefillin* on Ereb Yom Kippur, which many other Sephardim do not do. This is in order to show repentance for any negligence in connection with the *mizṿah* of *tefillin* before the Day of Atonement and to ask God for special forgiveness in this matter.

Teacher: When are *tefillin* generally taken off?

Student: Normally they shouldn't be taken off until after *Kaddish titkabal* and preferably not before *Kave el Hashem.* They should not be taken off in any event before the Torah has been read and they should not be taken off in the presence of one's rabbi or teacher. Rather one should go to the side to take them off in a private manner if it is before the end of the service. On the other hand, some like to study the *Ḥok Leyisrael* in the morning before removing their *tefillin,* if at all possible, so that they can have the *mizṿah* of studying Torah while wearing *tefillin.*

Teacher: Excellent! Thank you for a splendid answer! Now by the looks of these old *tefillin* that I have here as a sample for you, one can see that they have been around a long time and have stood up rather well. What is the normal procedure for investigating or inspecting the *tefillin* to see that they have not become *pasul*?

Student: Twice in seven years if one isn't wearing his *tefillin* regularly. Many people check them once a year during Ḥodesh Elul just to be fully certain they are *kasher.*

Teacher: Why do we take off the *tefillin shel rosh* before the *tefillin shel yad?* Who studied that assignment?

Student: Because so long as it says *totafot*, that means that the two *tefillin* must be on. Therefore we remove the *tefillin shel rosh* first and then the *tefillin shel yad,* while unwrapping the *reẓuot* (straps) around the hand in the middle of the process.

Teacher: Why are we supposed to touch our *tefillin* on both the arm and the head from time to time?

Student: All of us are familiar with the fact that a person usually touches his *tefillin* every once in a while as a reminder that he is wearing the *tefillin,* so that his thoughts and discussions should be of a holy nature. This is also done to make sure that the *tefillin* are in their proper place on the head and on the arm. Our rabbis have taught that it is a *segula* that one will be a *ben olam haba* if he checks on these matters carefully to show his love in the performance of this important *Miẓvah.* This is no easy task to constantly be aware that our thoughts and discussion should be directed in a manner of *kedushah* (holiness), which is probably why we no longer wear our *tefillin* all day long like they used to do in the olden times. Nowadays, things being as they are, we are best off removing the *tefillin* immediately after the morning service or after doing some learning in the *tefillin* during the day.

Teacher: I have a riddle or a question to ask for which you may or may not have the answer! You know, of course, that there are two *shins* on the *tefillin shel rosh,* one with three prongs and one with four prongs, which, as we have discussed in the past, are in order to fulfill the different ideas of how the *shin* should be made. For what other reason does the letter *shin* appear?

Student: It is because *shin* stands for 300, which is the exact number of days during the year when we put on *tefillin,* since the other days are Sabbaths and festivals.

Teacher: Wonderful! Well, all of you fellows will soon be approaching your Bar Miẓvah, and there are different customs as to when you should start to put on your *tefillin.* As you know, some of the Halakhah says that a young lad is able to put on *tefillin* as soon as he is old enough to be clean. Yet among the Syrians the *tefillin* are put on in the twelfth year, although a boy is not Bar Miẓvah until he is thirteen years and one day. Some groups have a longer training period than others. You, all of you, who are so well versed in the background in *tefillin,* I know that whatever is the particular custom in your family's tradition, certainly when you put on the *tefillin* they will surely direct the thoughts of your minds to holy things. You will also keep the intent of the word of God found in the four *parashiot* close to your heart because of the *shel yad.* This will make you think of God, and more than just thinking of Him, to perform in an active way the *Miẓvot* which the Torah requires of us. As you may know, the *Ḥayyei Abraham* brings the beautiful explanation of why there are four sections in the *tefillin shel rosh* and only one section or one opening in the *tefillin shel yad.* Rabbi Kalfon explains that we have our *four* senses in the head, those of sight, smell, hearing, and speaking, while in the hand we have only *one* sense, that of touch, through usage of the hand.

Class! Next lesson we will discuss at length exactly when each of you should begin to put on the *tefillin* in accordance with the calendar in preparation for your training for your Bar Miẓvah. Whatever that date will be, I know it should be a happy day for your parents because you are students who not only will put on *tefillin,* but based upon the fine manner in which you have studied the whole subject, it will be a *miẓvah* you will perform with love. It will bind you in the performance of the service of God in a way that will be an example to others. I am proud to be the teacher of such a fine class.

As you are about to leave, I would like you to take notice of these photographs which show the different ways that the Sephardim have for putting on the *tefillin,* as we have demonstrated. You will notice that the *shin dalet yod* are represented by some on the arm and on the hand in a different manner. Also note how the Ashkenazim do this by the spelling out of the *shin* on their hand in a manner different than the Sephardic way of the *shin* on the hand.

(A student is called up to demonstrate the Askenazic method of putting on *tefillin.*)

Teacher: How many of you already own *tefillin*? (Some students raise their hands.) Tell me, how far back do we know about the actual use of *tefillin* by our people?

Student: I have read that they found old parchments of *tefillin* in some of the archaeological digs in recent years and that there are photographs of those available in certain books. Could you possibly secure some of them so that we could look at them? Should I bring in the photographs of these old *tefillin*? I don't know how old they are, but I will check to see the date the book gives.

Teacher: Please do! Seeing is believing! All of us do believe, and it won't hurt us at all to see those ancient *tefillin.* The only thing that is different, I am sure, between them and ours today, is that today they are relatively more expensive. If you do not have a good pair of *tefillin* yet, prepare your parents to spend a goodly sum to buy you the finest possible *tefillin,* because you will be wearing them for the rest of your life!

Summary

As a follow-up on our discussion today I would like each of you to write a brief essay on how *tefillin* are worn in your specific community. Please describe the origin of the customs and state the date of your forthcoming thirteenth birthday so that we can plan for your "Day of *Tefillin*" and the date for your Bar Miẓvah. Shalom! Class is adjourned!

MODEL LESSON II

CYCLE I

ḤANUKKAH

(Reenactment of a class session)

Target Population

Class of either boys or girls. Upper grade in Yeshiva junior high or first grade of Yeshiva high school. The class has been prepared in advance by careful study of the sources.

Time

A period of fifty minutes (or two lessons of shorter duration).

INTRODUCTION

The teacher had given an advance assignment allocating different readings and sections of the study of the Halakhah and traditions of Ḥanukkah to all the members of the class. They had been given one week to review the material. The assignments allocated included readings from:

Shulḥan Arukh, Oraḥ Ḥayyim (671-684)
Kaf Haḥayyim (same chapters as listed above)
Mekor Ḥayyim Hashalem, Vol. IV (226-228)
Kiẓur Shulḥan Arukh Hashalem, Vol. II (234-247)
Ben Ish Ḥay, Shanah Rishona, Parashat Vayesheb
Yalkut Meam Loez, Bamidbar 101

This lesson was designed to be taught in either one or two parts depending upon the time schedule allocated by the individual junior high school for the study of *dinim* and *minhagim.* If taught in one session it would require the full fifty minutes. The lesson lent itself to being broken in the middle by the teacher with an appropriate summary which the teacher would have to improvise in a manner that would foretell the next series of topics to be discussed in the second part of the Ḥanukkah lesson. This lesson was presented to a class of boys.

OBJECTIVES OF THE LESSON WERE:

Informational

1. To quickly review the basic sources in: the Talmud (Tractate *Shabbat* 21b); *Mishneh Torah* of the Rambam, 1 Maccabees 1:10-16, 2 Maccabees 1; the Book of Judith; appropriate Midrashim found in *Midrash Leḥanukkah;* and in *Medrash Maase-Ḥanukkah* and in the fourth section of the Book of Josephus. All of the aforementioned sources were given as a prior class assignment for the class to review the history of the advent of the Ḥanukkah celebration so that this session was able to concentrate on the symbolism of the customs which appertain to the Ḥanukkah celebration. (A guide sheet seeking these objectives was distributed to accompany the homework assignment.)

Values

1. To communicate the essential victory of the Maccabees as having saved Torah life from complete destruction rather than just having won a military victory and to emphasize that this spiritual victory is responsible for the continuity of Jewish life until our very time.
2. To show the dedication of the Maccabees to the Land of Israel, which they loved, and for which they were ready to forfeit their lives, as a means of demonstrating the importance of love for the Land of Israel by Jews the world over.
3. A. To demonstrate the concept of the sanctification of God's name on earth by fighting to preserve the tenets of Torah life which the Hellenists and the Syrian-Greeks wished to obliterate in order to modernize Jewish life in accordance with the times and the philosophy of that era.
   B. To show their readiness to die *Al Kiddush Hashem* (to die

the death of holy martyrs) in a war which was waged to preserve these time-hallowed precepts of Torah as well as to save the physical land of Israel, even if it meant *fighting on the Sabbath* to save their lives (which had not been done before the time of the Maccabees).

4. To demonstrate how the specific observances of the Sephardic groups reflect and integrate into family life and Jewish community life the remembrance of the ideals which Ḥanukkah represents.
5. To relate the concept of Ḥanukkah (meaning "dedication"), which referred to the rededication of the Holy Temple, to the concept of *ḥinukh* (Jewish education) in order to show that both the worship of God through the offerings of sacrifice in olden times, the offering of prayer, and the study of Torah in our own day, are all important components to keep alive the light of the Jewish soul.

Diversified

1. To distinguish between Halakhah and *minhag hamakom,* and to define where *minhag bet ab* (family tradition) plays a role and what are its strengths and limits.
2. To highlight the important role that Jewish women have played throughout our history, as exemplified by Judith, Ḥannah, etc., who helped to perpetuate Jewish life and to secure our survival both physically and spiritually in yesteryear even as women still do today in the State of Israel.

Skills

To learn how to light Ḥanukkah lights and to observe Ḥanukkah according to different usages of the various communities.

MATERIALS

A. Use of overhead projector to exhibit and present photographs of a selection of rare *ḥanukkiyyot* showing the different Sephardic-type Ḥanukkah *menorot* of the various countries.

B. Students were asked to bring unique *ḥannukiyyot* from home to exhibit.

C. Museum books containing beautiful pictures of ancient *ḥanukkiyyot* borrowed from the Yeshiva University Museum were passed around the class.
D. Other materials should be Ḥanukkah candles and a can of olive oil for demonstration candle lighting and two *ḥanukkiyyot,* one for oil and one for candles, which will be used to kindle the lights.

METHODS

1. The various aspects of the Ḥanukkah victory were directly related to religious observances in order to emphasize their relevance to daily life today. For example, the miracle of the oil was emphasized by the presence and description and discussion relating to the lighting of the Ḥanukkah *menorot (ḥanukkiyyot)* either with oil or with candles. The spiritual victory for the survival of Torah was demonstrated through the celebration of the various *seudot* (banquets) arranged by the children in the community to mark Ḥanukkah as the time when funding for Jewish education was secured annually.
2. The important role of the women was mentioned in a special way and was designated by explaining the fact that women have been reserved a special place of honor in the celebration of Ḥanukkah. This is shown by the custom that they are to abstain from work during the time the Ḥanukkah candles are lit. The teacher questioned the class to determine the level of their knowledge of the various *minhagim* (customs) relating to Ḥanukkah to determine how well the class could make the connection between the various observances and the underlying important philosophical ideas and ideals which Ḥanukkah represents.

   The teacher tried to relate the different types of foods eaten and prepared for Ḥanukkah to the more significant symbolism which these gastronomic delights represent.

PRESENTATION (It should be noted that questions were always directed to the entire class. The teacher then called on specific students by name afterwards to give the answers. The presentation is rendered in the present tense to give the full flavor of the interaction.)

Teacher: I am sure that the various members of the class who undertook the different assignments have fulfilled their obligation and that I can now call upon you to give us a very brief synopsis of the various written sources for the Ḥanukkah observances. Who can please tell us where, and how, Ḥanukkah is mentioned in the Talmud?

Student: (He quotes the essential information from the Talmudic tractate *Shabbat* 21b, which emphasizes the miracle of the cruse of oil which burned for eight days.)

Teacher: Wonderful! Now who can tell us what the essential message of the Rambam (Maimonides) is in connection with the importance of the victory of the Maccabees over the Hellenists?

Student: The Rambam in *Mishneh Torah* emphasizes that it was this victory of a physical nature which enabled the Jews to continue to observe the study of Torah, the practice of circumcision, the preservation of Torah life as we know it today, etc. He points out that it was the Hasmonean priests who gave the leadership to the physical battle against the enemy even though one traditionally conceives of them only as spiritual-type leaders. He credits them with the restoration of the kingdom of Israel, which lasted until the destruction of the Second Temple in the year 70 of the common era.

Teacher: Great! Who knows what is the essential message that we learn from the Book of Maccabees?

Student: It basically describes the victory of Mattathias and his children in the battle of Modin which was the turning point in the victory of the Jews over the Syrian-Greeks.

Teacher: Dov! Your sister has been blessed with a special name of significance which relates to Ḥanukkah, and there is even a book of the Apocrypha in her name. Please summarize why her namesake, Judith, was so important to Ḥanukkah.

Student: (Dov tells of how Judith saved the Jews from Holfernes.)

Teacher: It is obvious that there were many miracles that took place of both a physical and spiritual nature during that period in Jewish history which we commemorate with our eight-day celebration of Ḥanukkah. How do we express this thanksgiving in our prayer services?

Student: During the Ḥanukkah holiday, every day at the services we add *Al hanisim* in the *Amidah* (as well as in the *Birkat Hamazon),* we recite the complete *Hallel* from beginning to end, we take out the *Sefer Torah* and read from *Parashat Hanesiyim* (Numbers 7), reading a section each day.

Teacher: What do we do on Rosh Ḥodesh Tebet, which falls during the week? Please give all the details!

Student: We pray like on every Rosh Ḥodesh and add *Yaaleh veyabo,* recite *Al hanisim,* the complete *Hallel,* and we take out two *Sifrei Torah.* In the first we read *Parashat Rosh Ḥodesh* (Numbers 28), and in the second *Sefer* we read *Parashat Hanesiyim* (Numbers 7). We then add the *Musaf* of Rosh Ḥodesh, and of course we remember to include *Al hanisim.*

Teacher: Well, it would seem that the years of experience that our class has had shows us to be quite expert in the expression of the prayers. Tell me, what happens on Shabbat Ḥanukkah?

Student: In the regular Shabbat service, during the *Amidah* we say *Al hanisim.* We then recite the complete *Hallel,* and take out two *Sifrei Torah.* In the first we read from the weekly portion and call seven, and from the second *Sefer* we call the *maftir* in *Parashat Hanesiyim* and we read *Rani vesimḥi* (Zekhariah 2:14-4:7). When we are blessed with two Shabbatot on Ḥanukkah, we recite the *maftir* on the second Shabbat, derived from 1 Kings 7:40-50, pray the *Musaf* as on other Sabbaths, and of course include *Al hanisim.*

Teacher: There are two Shabbatot throughout the year when three *Sifrei Torah* are taken from the *heikhal!* When are they?

Student: One is on the Sabbath of Rosh Ḥodesh which is also Ḥanukkah. It is literally a full house in terms of the *simḥa* it brings through the recitation of the Sabbath *Amidah* with *Yaaleh veyabo, Al hanisim,* the recitation of the complete *Hallel,* and the taking of three *Sifrei Torah.* In the first we read the *Parashat Hashabua,* from the second we read *Parshat Rosh Ḥodesh,* from *Beyom Hashabbat* until *Venisko,* and from the third we read *maftir* from *Parashat Hanesiyim* and we recite the Haftarah, *Rani vesimḥi* (Zekhariah 2:14-4:17). Some have the custom to add to the Haftarah on the Shabbat of Rosh Ḥodesh and Ḥanukkah the first verse and the last verse from the Haftarah, *Hashamayim Kisi* (Isaiah 66), which is normally said on Shabbat Rosh Ḥodesh. Of course in the *Musaf* both *Ata Yaẓarta* and *Al hanisim* are recited. The other time three *Sifrei Torah* are taken out is Rosh Ḥodesh Nisan, *Parashat Haḥodesh* (or Rosh Ḥodesh Adar II, which is *Parashat Shekalim).*

Teacher: Well, I must say that you are all pretty good. But complete perfection is still a goal to be achieved. What other significant differences in the Syrian services have not yet been mentioned?

Student: Well, there is the standard tradition not to begin the *Mizmor Shir Ḥanukkat Habayit leDavid* after *Hodu* in the weekday and Sabbath *Shaḥarit* services, where the prayer begins with *Aromimekha Hashem ki dilitani* by the Syrian community as a special remembrance of the destruction of the Temple. Instead they say this prayer immediately after the *Sefer* is returned to the Ark.

Teacher: That is really an interesting custom which obviously is observed only by the Aleppo Jews, who wished to thereby indicate that the Temple dedicated in the time of the Hasmoneans had not yet been rebuilt. This custom is different, you know, than that of the other Sephardic groups, who always replace the *Shir shel yom* (daily Psalm) with the *Mizmor Shir Ḥanukkat Habayit leDavid* throughout the Ḥanukkah celebration, whereas they normally leave out this first line and begin with *Aromimekha Hashem ki dilitani.* How do we thank God for the essence of the Ḥanukkah miracle?

Student: The most significant way that we express thanksgiving for Ḥanukkah is by the lighting of the Ḥanukkah candles each night and at synagogue services each evening and morning!

Teacher: Correct! Although we have not yet discussed this fully, I am sure we all bear it in mind as the focal point of the expression of thanksgiving on Ḥanukkah. Since we are now focusing on that, I would like to ask you what are the blessings that we recite on the first night of Ḥanukkah?

Student: It is our custom in the Syrian community to recite the first blessing, *Barukh . . . lehadlik ner Ḥanukkah.* We then light the candle with the recitation of the second blessing, *Barukh . . . she-asa nisim laaboteinu,* followed by the third blessing of *Sheheḥeyanu.* Ḥabad Ḥassidim do the same.

Teacher: That is very interesting. As you know the Ashkenazim and the Spanish and Portuguese Jews as well recite the first blessing as *Barukh . . . lehadlik ner shel Ḥanukkah!* Why do you think Ḥassidim and Sephardic groups omit the word *shel?*

(No one was able to give the proper answer, although attempts were made by various students.)

Teacher: The real answer is that since it is forbidden to use the lights of the Ḥanukkah candle, the blessing excludes the word *shel.* We include the word *shel* when we are permitted to make use of the light, such as on the Sabbath or on festivals when we say *Lehadlik ner shel Shabbat,* or *Lehadlik ner shel Yom Tob.* Now let me ask you a question which may make you think a little: How many candles do you light on the first night of Ḥanukkah, and how many on the second night of Ḥanukkah? Describe the actual ceremony!

Student: On the first night we light the *shamash* with which we light the first candle, placing it at the right hand side of the *menorah.* On the second night we put the two candles into the *menorah,* placing the first candle furthest right and second candle to its left. We then light the second candle first and then the first candle.

Teacher: Does everybody agree that this is the way it must be done? Have any of you ever seen it done in another manner?

Student: Yes, I have seen it done in the following manner, which is different than that which has just been described. First of all, the *shamash* is lit with a candle which is a tapered long candle and then the Ḥanukkah candles or oil wicks are lit. It is not our tradition in the Syrian community to use the *shamash* to light the other candles or wicks. We keep it there solely to protect the Ḥanukkah lights from being used or from in any way having benefit derived from their light, which is forbidden. Instead any benefit which might be given off by the lights is attributed to the light derived from the *shamash*. In this way we do not transgress the law not to benefit from the light of the Ḥanukkah candles, which must simply be used for the purpose of *pirsumei nisa* (the public proclamation of the great miracle of Ḥanukkah which God performed for the Jewish people).

Teacher: I remember seeing something that struck me as being rather different, something unique. One Ḥanukkah when I visited the home of one of my Syrian friends, I noticed that in addition to lighting the *shamash* on the first night, the family lit two candles on the first night. I was told when I asked *why* they light an additional candle that they do this each night, which would mean that on the second night in addition to the *shamash* they would light three candles, on the third night four candles, etc. The whole thing seemed rather confusing, and nobody really understood why this was being done except that it was their family tradition from generation to generation. I would love to know if anyone else has ever seen this kind of candlelighting ceremony and if you know the reason for it? Does anyone know the answer?

(Class is silent.)

Teacher: Here, we have come across one of the most unique traditions in the Sephardic community in connection with candlelighting. These people were descendants of a Spanish family who had made their ultimate way from Spain to Syria in the sixteenth century and who offered thanksgiving to the Almighty that their community (which had not been too readily accepted into the indigenous Syrian community), was finally officially accepted into full membership of the Syrian community on Ereb Ḥanukkah, at that time. In order to commemorate the celebration of their acceptance into the community, and as an expression of additional thanksgiving to the Almighty, those exiled Spanish Jews added an extra candle each of the eight nights of Ḥanukkah because they were so grateful for having been accepted by the native Syrian community who were known as *Mustarabim*. This is a very interesting point in Jewish history which reflects upon the long controversy that extended between the Spanish-Syrian community and the indigenous community, which was finally resolved. Therefore, families which stem from Spanish origins have perpetuated the tradition even though many of them do not really understand why they are doing so! How do the Jews of Damascus light the Ḥanukkah lights?

Student: Well, I would just like to say that among our Damascene Jews things are much less confusing and we simply light a *shamash* and add an additional candle for each night of Ḥanukkah, much like the Ashkenazim.

Teacher: What other prayers do you recite after lighting the candles?

Student: On the first night we recite *Lehadlik ner Ḥanukkah,* as we have already explained, plus the second blessing, *Sheasa nisim laaboteinu bayamim hahem bazeman hazeh,* plus the third blessing, *Sheheḥeyanu*. After that we sing the *Mizmor shir Ḥanukkat habayit*.

Student: In our house we also sing the *Maoz ẓur* even though we are Syrians. It seems that this must be a custom that has been adopted since our people came to America, since I have been told that the *Maoz ẓur* is of Eastern European origin.

Teacher: What you say is probably true. It is also interesting to note that the Spanish and Portuguese Jews, who do not recite the *Maoz ẓur,* do, nevertheless, use its melody in the chanting of the *Ein k-Elokeinu* at the conclusion of their services during Ḥanukkah. I also would like to point out that it seems to be a custom in most Sephardic homes to use oil in preference to candles. However, I recently read about an interesting custom of the Jews of Izmir, who kept the leftover *candles* that they used during the Ḥanukkah celebration and used these to burn the *ḥameẓ* on Passover, which must mean that candles were also used. Now, tell me, *do girls have to light* the Ḥanukkah lights?

Student: Yes! Absolutely! Girls should be taught that it is a commandment for them to light the Ḥanukkah candles just as well as it is an obligation incumbent upon the men, and if they are away from home, at school or elsewhere where they are not fulfilling the *miẓvah* through the lighting of the candles by their father, they have the obligation, according to the *Shulḥan Arukh, Oraḥ Ḥayyim* to kindle the Ḥanukkah candles!

Teacher: What are the different customs in connection with this whole idea of where to place the *ḥanukkiyiah?* Why do some people place it in the window, while others place the *ḥanukkiyiah* on the doorpost at the entrance of their home opposite the *mezuzah?* Which is correct?

Student: Both are correct, since the customs were derived from the different communities in which the people lived. Because we today want to give maximum exposure to proclaim the miracle, many of us place the *ḥanukkiyiah* in the window. This is not meant to emulate our Christian neighbors, who put up wreaths and other insignias to celebrate their major festival, which falls at the same season. It is simply because it is felt that this will allow the Ḥanukkah lights to be seen by the largest number of persons. In the olden days in many communities, the most appropriate place to achieve this was in the entrance way, since people came into your house and would immediately notice the Ḥanukkah lights, thereby giving proclamation to the miracle in the fullest. One would also be surrounded by the *mezuzah* on the one side and the lights on the other, so that he would have the *mizvot* encompass him on both sides as he came and left his house.

Teacher: What's the mystique of the *Hanerot halalu* prayer recited after the candlelighting? (Silence prevails.) It's a numerical mystique. (Silence persists.) A hint is that all through *Sefirat Haomer* we say *Lamenazzeaḥ binginot* because it has forty-nine words. (Pause by teacher.) Well, since you can't guess I'll tell you *the long* and *the short* of it! There are two versions of *Hanerot halalu* — long and short! In most of the Sephardic communities they recite the shorter one, which besides the first two words, *Hanerot halalu,* includes thirty-six words, which is exactly the same as the number of lights or candles kindled during the eight-day Ḥanukkah period!

Well, I guess another Ḥanukkah miracle is that nobody yet has asked about the tremendous oil consumption in the preparation of the special foods we enjoy so much during the Ḥanukkah celebration. How do your families prepare these delicacies?

Student: My mother has a specialty of making *sufganiyot,* which are a type of jelly donut deep-fried in oil. They are surely not low on the calorie count, and if everyone in Temple times was making similar delicacies they were lucky not to run out of oil again!

Student: I once visited with a Moroccan family during Ḥanukkah, and I noticed that they served a special meal with couscous and a rooster. It was delicious! They said they used a rooster because the miracle of Ḥanukkah was brought about by a male, Judah the Maccabee!

Student: My mother is Turkish, and I defy anybody to come up with a delicacy that tastes better than her *buermuelos,* which are puff-like fritters which are deep-fried in oil. It is dipped in honey syrup and then sprinkled with sugar powder and cinnamon, and it sure is a specialty that I think about all year.

Teacher: I have an idea of how we can get to taste some of these goodies! Who knows what a *merenda* is?

Student: Among the Turkish Jews on the last day of Ḥanukkah, they observe what is known as the *merenda*, or "pot-luck picnic." Indeed, how about each of us who have strictly kasher homes bringing in some food that represents a specialty that our family makes for Ḥanukkah so that we can have one big party here in the class that will be a *merenda* party. Of course, at home at the conclusion of the *merenda* all the children receive money as gifts for Ḥanukkah, which I believe has been the tradition in most communities. But don't worry, dear teacher, we will forego that part of the celebration if the class agrees to hold a *merenda!*

Teacher: Well, let's have a show of hands as to how many of you would like to either prepare by yourselves, or ask your mothers to prepare, some strictly kasher specialties so that we can have a *merenda* and celebrate the last day of Ḥanukkah in class? (All hands go up.) The overwhelming response makes for an immediate decision that such a concluding *merenda* party will be held!

(Teacher concludes the lesson here with a brief summary if the lesson is divided into two sessions.)

(Second session or continuation of first lesson.)

Teacher: You know the idea of having a party for ourselves is really in keeping with an ancient Jewish tradition of Ḥanukkah. In fact, it was the Jews in Damascus who really instituted these special three meals *(seudot)* in connection with Ḥanukkah. And it was their children who took the lead in setting up the whole procedure. As you know, Ḥanukkah relates to the Hebrew word *ḥinukh*, which means "education." Therefore, the children would go around collecting from house to house singing from the Biblical quote found in *Parashat Mikeẓ: Shubu shibru lanu meat okhel* (Genesis 43:2) — "Go again, buy us a little food." When so requested by the children, each family would respond with a generous gift of food or money to provide food. These monies and foods were accumulated and distributed to the teachers, and this constituted the basis for their salary for the year. Both in food and money, their security for the entire year was assured by this communal effort led by the children in the community so that Jewish education *(ḥinukh)* would be secure. In addition a special banquet was held in honor of the teachers to show respect to them and to show respect for the Torah which they taught.

Another banquet which would be funded by the same gifts given from the door-to-door solicitation by the children would be for the poor of the city for whom a very special spread was made, and the rabbis and lay leaders of the community would attend this occasion in order to give a feeling of honor and recognition to the poor who attended. What was another *seudah* which the students held?

Student: A third *seudah* was held for the children themselves with whatever funds they could scrape together after having accomplished the two other banquets which were for the benefit of the community. All of this was done in Damascus as a part of the Ḥanukkah tradition.

Teacher: I think it is beautiful that our holidays emphasize and make sure that the needs of others are taken into consideration. Recently, I read that the Judeo-Spanish Jews consider the Sabbath of Ḥanukkah as Shabbat Hahalbashah (the Sabbath for collecting clothing for the needy). Who can tell me about it?

Student: The rabbi speaks to the congregation about the need to provide proper clothing at this season for the poor and the elderly. Thank God, not too many people need this kind of help in our own society today, but in communities such as Salonika and in the other "Old Country" communities, it was nice to know that at the time of lighting candles our people thought of providing warmth and security during the inclement weather of winter, for the poor and the needy as well.

Teacher: I can't think of a better way to conclude our lesson than to remind you that the joy we bring to others is often the greatest joy we experience for ourselves. Ḥanukkah has been symbolic of the survival of the Jewish people because of the miracle of the cruse of oil and because in every generation Jews have been willing to fight for our self-preservation and our continuity. We remember our hard times by games such as the *dreydl,* or *sevivon,* and other games of chance which make Ḥanukkah money gifts and other gifts a source of pleasure for us to take as we recall sadder times gone by. We remember the poor, we pay tribute to our teachers, and we celebrate ourselves. I ask that besides bringing in your goodies, you should also bring in a complete array of the traditional riddles which used to be asked in the Sephardic communities during Ḥanukkah; that you come prepared to entertain us with the singing of some *piyutim* that were among the Ḥanukkah specials, such as *Imru l'Elokim, Hayom hazeh, Shabbat veḥanukkah,* and *Ikhlu mishmanim.* Please prepare these well, for they will be as much fun as the eating!

You will recall that at the beginning of our lesson, I pointed out to you these various unique *ḥanukkiyyot* (candelabra for Ḥanukkah) which have been photographed from the collections of several outstanding Jewish museums. What makes each of these Ḥanukkah *menorot (ḥanukkiyyot)* so special?

Student: Each reflects the craftsmanship, the materials, and the manner in which *hiddur miẓvah* (special loving care given to the performance of a commandment) was enacted by the artisans who made them.

(Here the teacher uses an overhead projector or slide projector to show pictures of unique old and interesting *ḥanukkiyyot.*)

Teacher: Some are very ancient and thus very crude. Others really represent the finest in workmanship in silver and gold. Others are made of various kinds of metals combined with glass to protect the wicks in the oil. Each of them tells you something about the community that you might want to look into. Yes, you have your hand up, what is it?

Student: It seems the one thing that all these *menorot* have in common is that they commemorate an event that took place in *Ereẓ Yisrael.* While we have talked about so many aspects of the holiday, we should not lose sight of the fact that the entire celebration was due to the heroic efforts of the Maccabees and the Hasmoneans who fought for the preservation of Jewish spiritual life and for the survival of the Land of Israel as the national home of the Jewish people.

Teacher: As we celebrate Ḥanukkah here in America and when a Jew in any part of the world lights the candles, his heart must turn to Jerusalem and to the place where it all occurred. On the *dreydl* (which Ashkenazim use to play gambling games on Ḥanukkah), the letters *nun, gimel, heh, shin* designate the well-known statement *Nes Gadol Hayah Sham* (a great miracle happened *there).* If we commemorate the miracle without thinking about *where* it took place and do not consider our own love and attachment to the Land of Israel, we are ignoring an essential element of the miracle of Jewish survival, which has always centered around the eternal love of the Jewish people for the Land of Israel.

Student: I would like to make the following suggestion. Since we have agreed to hold our next lesson on Ḥanukkah, as a special *seudah* (banquet) in the spirit of the *merenda* and the banquets we have discussed which provided financial support for the study of Torah, which provided for the needy, and which also provided respect for teachers of Torah, I would humbly suggest that our banquet could also include a brief session of games of chance. Each of us should come ready to make a contribution that will be sent to *Ereẓ Israel.* The money that we play with, whether we win or lose, will, at the end of the session, be contributed to the Land of Israel. What kinds of institutions in Israel do you think should be the recipients of the contributions we will make?

Student: Well, it appears from what we have said that the victory of the Maccabees was fought by Jews who were willing to sacrifice their lives to secure the Land of Israel as well as to secure its holiness and the religious observances which were enacted in the Temple. If it is all right with the rest of the class, I would like to suggest that some of the money which will be accumulated from our *seudah* and our games should be sent to a Yeshibat Hesder in the State of Israel run by the Benei Akiba organization. The reason I suggest this type of institution is because the young men who go into the army spend a half day learning Torah each day and a half day in military service. They have been among the most valiant and courageous fighters in the most dangerous areas in recent years. Don't you agree that those students who study Torah, and who have financial needs and who have teachers who are devoting themselves in a similar fashion by combining the weaponry of Torah and the implements of war to secure the borders and the Land of Israel, that this kind of institution should receive some of our support?

Teacher: Well, I agree to put forward this proposal of Yehuda's. Are there any other ideas that any of you may wish to entertain along these lines?

Student: It seems that Yehuda has hit the nail on the head! That does not mean that I have made him a *maccabee* (hammer)! (This may be accepted as a joke in the class.) However, all the elements of what the victory of the Ḥanukkah story represents are truly encompassed in the group of young men (who are also supported by young women of like mind) attending the Hesder Yeshibot in Israel. I would ask the class to acclaim its support for these institutions to receive a good portion of our funds.

(The teacher asks for a raise of hands of all in favor and with only one or two exceptions, everybody is in agreement.)

Summary by Teacher

You know, I think we have accomplished a great deal today. In our earlier years Ḥanukkah meant something special to us, as it does to all Jewish young people everywhere. It is exciting, however, to notice the inner personal and spiritual growth that each of us has been able to express as we mature and look upon Ḥanukkah from a different perspective each year. However, I would like to point out that even when we speak the truth about someone who is not doing something right, it is considered to be *lashon harah* (slander). Yes, indeed, because even some of the best-intentioned statements of people come under the category of *slander,* the Syrian Jewish community has, together with other Sephardic communities, such as Morocco and elsewhere, over the years, observed a special *taanit dibbur* (a fast-day of silence, which is marked on the day after "Rosh Ḥodesh Shebat"). It was interesting to receive a letter from Chief Rabbi Jacob S. Kassin of the Brooklyn Syrian community only a few years ago, urging communities throughout the land to reinstitute and to reinforce the enactment of this ancient Jewish tradition. On this day which calls upon people to refrain from speaking and to completely dedicate themselves to meditation and to the study of Torah as a means of doing *teshuba* (repentance) for the sin of slander *(lashon harah)* of which everyone is guilty at some time of the year, the entire Book of *Tehillim* (Psalms) is read three times.

Surely all of us can recognize that the light of Torah which Ḥanukkah represents, which *ḥinukh* (Jewish education) symbolizes, and which our observances hope to inspire, seek to make us better people both in the things that we do and the things we ought not to do.

I look forward to our next class and I invite all of you to carefully view the *ḥanukkiyyot* on display as well as to bring in the song, spirit, and joy about which we have spoken at our next Ḥanukkah lesson. Also please copy the following homework assignment in your notebooks:

I would like each member of the class to provide me with a half-page description of whatever food they will contribute to our party next week, indicating its symbolic significance relative to the celebration of Ḥanukkah. That is your homework assignment.

Shalom!

(The Class is adjourned.)

MODEL LESSON III

CYCLE III

SELECTION OF A MATE, ENGAGEMENT, AND MARRIAGE

Lesson I

(A lesson in two sessions)

(Reenactment of classroom session)

Target Population

A class of senior Yeshiva high school girls.

Time

A period of fifty minutes.

OBJECTIVES

Educational and Values

1. To impart the idea that the selection of a proper mate in life for the purpose of Jewish marriage is of utmost importance because in Judaism marriage is essential to Jewish continuity and the eternity of the Jewish people.
2. To instill the concept of *ẓeniut* (Jewish modesty and refinement) because marriage by definition of its Hebrew name, *Kiddushin* (marriage), implies that the relationship between husband and wife is something holy, exclusive, and special, which from the Torah viewpoint makes it an essential element of holiness in God's plan for the creation of the Children of Israel to be a "holy people and a kingdom of priests."

3. To create an implicit understanding that in Judaism marriage and procreation are one and the same, and that both the elements of personal fulfillment and happiness of the individuals marrying as mates and companions, and their ability to secure the continuity of Jewish life through procreation are all important elements in *Kiddushin*—the holy union of marriage.
4. That the goal of a Torah-trained girl or boy should be to so live their lives in their youth that the stamp of *kedushah* (holiness) should be one which they will bring to their ultimate *Kiddushin* (marriage). This is achieved by conducting themselves in a disciplined manner according to the instructions of the Torah and Sages, as communicated by parents, teachers, and the written word, as regards Jewish modesty and a social lifestyle which is in consonance with the upright conduct of social life expected of *Benei Torah* in our society.

MATERIALS

Wedding invitation with many adjectives extolling the bride and groom as pious and learned young people.
Copy of a Syrian *Ketubbah*

METHOD

1. The teacher motivated the class to a discussion on the question of selecting a proper mate by advising them that he has just received a wedding invitation from a former student (possibly the sister of one of the girls present in the class) whom he had been privileged to teach only three years ago. She has since graduated from the school and had recently become engaged to a young *Ben Torah* who has been studying at Yeshiva University (or at any other appropriate school of special significance to the group) where he has been deeply involved in Torah studies while preparing for a professional career in the field of Jewish service (as a rabbi, as an educator, or as a social worker, etc.). By use of this example and a discussion of what a wonderful match

the young couple are for one another, the teacher, through the inquiry method, and through the discussion method, determined the thinking, the level of knowledge of the important rabbinic and Torah precepts involved, and offered examples through quotations from appropriate Torah and rabbinic sources to impart additional knowledge in order to help formulate positive attitudes and opinions on the question of selecting a proper mate for marriage.

2. At the conclusion of this session, which was primarily used to set the stage for discussion on the social setting of young people, the values they should espouse and be seeking in potential mates, and in discussing other problems relating to contemporary views of marriage which are contrary to the traditional Torah views, the teacher set the stage for *Lesson Two,* which empirically demonstrated through the customs of the marriage ceremony the significance of the matters under discussion in *Lesson One.* Members of the class were asked to interview two couples as a follow-up of this lesson.

PRESENTATION BY TEACHER (presented in the present tense to give the full flavor of the interaction)

Scenario of Discussion between Teacher and Students.

1. The teacher welcomes the class with a bright smile on his face, holding in his hand a wedding invitation which he describes to the girls in the class, who are all very curious as to who is about to get married. He indicates that Sarah Levi, a former student of his (optional: whose sister is in the class) had just sent him and his wife this invitation to participate in the joyous occasion of her forthcoming marriage to Ben Zion Cohen, a third year *semikhah* student at the Rabbi Isaac Elchanan Theological Seminary of Yeshiva University (or any other seminary appropriate and of significance to the group of girls with whom this is being discussed) while she was herself completing her bachelor's degree at Stern College for Women and was planning to go into the field of Jewish education. He had since learned that the *ḥatan* (groom) upon completion of his *semikhah* (rabbinic

ordination) was planning to enter into the field of Jewish education as a teacher, with a view to ultimately become an administrator. The teacher comments on his great joy that this young couple have found each other, have a common interest in their desire to be of service to the Jewish community, and from what he understands of their respective families, each brings with them the family *yiḥus* of note which augers well for a fine Jewish marriage which will hopefully result in the building of a loyal Jewish home. He expresses the hope that their marriage will be fruitful and that through their marriage they will continue to build Jewish life for generations to come.

(The teacher passes the invitation around the class for the girls to see. It is a beautifully engraved invitation in Hebrew and in English in the finest format of current invitations presently being used in the Torah community.)

Having made his comment that the couple was so well matched for one another based upon their similiar educational backgrounds, their professional interests, and their family backgrounds, the teacher stops to allow the girls in the class, some of whom know the bride and one or two of whom also know the groom, to make comments about them. (Or teacher describes her background and then asks questions to stimulate discussion of this type.)

Student: Sarah was always the studious kind of *Bat Torah* who would seek a husband whose interests would be in continuing to learn Torah and to teach Torah to others as well. Her own academic achievements while in this school, about which we have heard from friends who know her well, show that she is one of the truly fine girls that have gone through our school and I think that we can all be proud of her own attainments and be happy for her that she has found this kind of *zivug* (match)!

Another student comments:

After hearing about the outstanding accomplishments of Sarah as leader of the Dramatics Society when she was in our school, it is no wonder that she has chosen to pursue a career as a teacher. She will obviously be a wonderful teacher of Judaism, and she is so fortunate that she has found a mate whose life's ambitions are so in line with her own. That will allow her to give full expression to her talents and to her desire to be of service to the Jewish people.

A third student states:

The *ḥatan* seems to be a young man who is not only diligent in his own Torah studies but has undertaken a special obligation to spend extra time in tutoring other students at Yeshiva who are weak in their Talmudic studies and who need the *ḥizzuk* which he can provide for them. From everything that I have heard about him he will be a marvelous educator and his sense of commitment is such that I understand that he is willing (and she too) to go out of town to help strengthen the smaller communities and to build a new Yeshiva. That needs this kind of young couple who are deeply committed to *yahadut*.

Teacher: Well, from what you girls say, this does seem to be one of the finest matches, and since we believe that *Hashem mezaveg zivugim* (that God helps to bring couples together who are well suited for one another), the question that we must ask ourselves is: how do we go about meeting young people who have the interests, backgrounds, and ideals similar to ours, which can make for the kind of *shiddukh* that we are all so elated about here this morning? Even though we believe that marriages may be made in heaven, I would like to suggest that the concept of *ozov taazov imo* (God helps those who are in the process of trying to help themselves) applies here. What set of conditions, what kinds of organizations, what kind of social contacts can bring together young people who share ideals and lifestyles that can bring about the kind of *shiddukhim* that all of us know make for the happy and sustained marriages that have built generations of Jews? The role of the *shadkhan*, while it was quite popular until recently, and may still be a viable approach in some small select communities, has for the most part disappeared. That means that self-selection of mates becomes an obligation upon each one of you and those with whom you socialize. Where and how do you go about meeting such people? What are some of the problems that exist in the community which sometimes make it difficult for good matches to be made, so that we sometimes have wonderful observant girls who may end up settling for less in their husband than they would originally have hoped to settle for? Just as we are elated over the forthcoming marriage of Sarah and Ben Zion, I can tell you about another wonderful girl in this school (whose name I will naturally withhold), who married somebody who was *not* a proper match for her, simply because she was so taken in by the prestige of the out-of-town graduate school that he attended and his preparing for the particular lucrative and prestigious profession for which he was studying. Many other girls have married *Benei Torah* who practice that same profession, who attended an excellent local school, but have instead never severed their study of Torah or have never left the Torah milieu while seeking to prepare themselves for a profession!

Student: It is important to socialize within the context of organizations that bring together like-minded people, with similar backgrounds and who are themselves looking for a spouse who will bring the background of Torah learning, Torah ideals, and other matters of common interest with them into the social setting. There are only a select number of places where these young people can meet within appropriate social settings where they can have some kind of contact, while always remembering the restrictions and the limitations that our Torah imposes upon us in developing and nurturing relationships and friendships that could, hopefully, lead to marriage.

Teacher: What you are saying, then, is that a girl or boy who is of Torah vintage has to conduct herself or himself in a certain disciplined manner! Let us be specific, and let us openly speak about the kinds of conduct we expect of boys and girls in the various social settings, whether they be at seminars, social weekends under proper supervision, or at intellectual gatherings, etc. How do you actually conduct yourselves?

Student: All of us know that the separation of the sexes before marriage is required within the context of our Torah heritage. We are also aware that *yiḥud* is forbidden. Therefore the concept of "safety in numbers" and the congeniality of larger social gatherings is the best kind of place where we can meet the prospective young men. If we are working together in projects such as Torah Leadership Seminars or other outreach programs, working with respective groups of boys and girls, and coming together on certain occasions, this allows us to be able to see and take note of the type of personalities that are involved before we even begin to have what might be called "personal conversations" with them.

Teacher: What you are saying is so true! We learn from the very *Birkat erusin* (blessings of marriage) that there are *two* things which we discern from these blessings, namely, that there should be *kedushah* (holiness) because God is *mekadesh amo Yisrael bikidushin* (God sanctifies His people through marriage) and He also has *forbidden* us the *arayiot* (forbidden relationships). What would be considered as *arayiot*? Does this only mean a forbidden relationship between unmarried people? Or does it also mean that certain relatives and certain people within the Jewish community are forbidden to marry one another?

Student: Obviously, *arayiot* means that none of the forbidden familial, incestuous relations are allowed. In the broader sense it also means that a *kohen* may not marry a divorcee or a convert, although we know he may marry a widow.

Student: In a real larger context for *us*, the meaning of *arayiot* is living in this terribly sensuous and promiscuous society which makes it very hard for a *Bat Torah* to socialize without being made to feel like a wallflower and to feel very different. The manner in which we are prepared to speak to a member of the opposite sex, immediately presents problems of communication and makes it more difficult to get to know someone.

Teacher: What you have said is a fact! Today there are no bounds in society. Many of our very fine people who have attained affluence and a high position in society in recent years have come to think that one has to be a part of the "social jet set," of the "disco scene," the social clubs, the swimming clubs and country clubs, in order to be an acceptable member of high society. Fortunately, we have our own "high society," which is on a higher standard than those I have just described. When it states, *Umotar ha-adam min habehemah ayin,* most people understand this to mean that "the difference between man and animal is nought." The truth is that the animal kingdom and man have all been given certain instincts, drives, *needs,* and both have a strong desire to fulfill these needs. However, the difference between the animal kingdom and man (who is rational) is God's gift to man to be able to say *"Ayin"*—NO! This exercise of a higher discipline enables him or her to overcome the temptations of the moment in order to retain the state of purity that will ultimately be shared in *Kiddushin* with a fine Jewish spouse of a similar conviction. Who knows what the most difficult laws were for the Jews to accept when God conferred the 613 commandments at Mount Sinai?

(After the students try to answer, the likelihood is that few will know the true answer.)

Teacher: The answer is, *Beshaah sheniẓtavu benei Yisrael al ha-arayiot bakhu vekiblu miẓvah zu betarumot ubekhiah, sheneemar bokheh lemishpeḥotov al iskei mishpaḥot* (Numbers 11:10 and the commentary by *Sifri,* as well as Rambam, *Hilkhot Isurei Biya* 22:8). This *maamar ḥazal* is enough to show us how natural and prevalent these attractions and temptations are, and always were. That is why we have to be extremely cautious and to exercise the qualities of Torah discipline which we are privileged to share and to strengthen one another in a milieu which will accept our "prudish," but refined, Torah-oriented views about social contact. Obviously, therefore, the kinds of places to which young men and women go should be those where they know they will find like-minded individuals lest they be faced with the temptation of confronting and encountering individuals whose lifestyle and whose ideals will not be in consonance with our own true inner souls.

In addition to these qualities we have discussed, what importance should be attached to family *yiḥus* (family pedigree)?

(By listening to the answers of the students the teacher discovers some of the elements of their understanding of the importance of the role of this concept. He should interject to show how, through the generations, great Jewish families have been preserved. Their examples of devotion to Torah living have come down to this day because the families were careful to select each other and because they shared the same value systems of one another.)

Teacher: How should a *Baal Teshubah* (a bonafide *Ben Torah* whose commitment to Judaism was only recently acquired) be looked upon? This is a basic question to be discussed today, since so many of our Yeshivot for both boys and girls have succeeded in attracting the hearts and minds of fine young Jews who are *ḥozrim beteshubah* and who can now begin to rebuild a lineage of Torah-true Jews?

(Here the teacher and the students should be encouraged to quote and research sources of the Bible, Talmud, Midrash and *Halakhah* which will support the point of view that they espouse. In general, an encouragement for positive acceptance of serious *Baalei Teshubah,* who are truly convinced, learned, and observant Jews who have superseded the observance of their parents, should be given very special consideration.)

(The concept of checking into family backgrounds in today's helter-skelter society when the sanctity of Jewish life is imperiled by the disorganization, is a factor that should be emphasized. Especially at this time when patrilineal Jews and quickie non-halakhic conversions abound.)

Teacher: Having discussed the qualities of the kind of person we would like to share our lives with, I must now ask a basic question from a Torah perspective. What is the primary purpose of marriage?

Student: We are told the first *mizvah* in the Torah is *peru urebu* (Multiply and be fruitful), which means that *procreation* is the primary purpose of marriage.

Teacher: Do you feel that this concept is accepted even by all of our own fine young daughters, some of whom may have been persuaded by the notions in today's modern society that it is more important to have a fulfilling career, or by some of the other persuasive women's-lib arguments which obviously are at loggerheads with the primary *mizvah* of "Multiply and be fruitful"?

(The girl students will have much to say on this, but after all has been said there will be an agreement that Jewish continuity and the eternity of the Jewish people can only be preserved by the fulfillment of procreation. If a family is not continued, its place in Judaism is lost forever and generations will go unborn who would otherwise have carried on the message that has come from the time of Abraham, through Sinai, to our own day.)

Teacher: Perhaps, if you really understand that procreation and that the raising of a family is a major and primary purpose of marriage, you will be a little more understanding of why there are certain groups of Jews, certain Sephardic communities, which in the Old Country (and this of course does not appertain to North America, where bigamy is prohibited by civil law) had a condition in the *ketubbah* (marriage contract) which was actually recorded in halakhah, that if the marriage was barren after a period of ten years, the husband could divorce the woman (in which case both she and he could remarry and perhaps be successful in raising a family with a spouse with whom they would be more physically compatible from the standpoint of having children.) Some *ketubbot* stipulate that under such conditions the husband could, with the consent of his wife, take a second wife for the purpose of raising a family to perpetuate his family's name. Were you aware of the fact that a *ketubbah* could contain such a condition? Are you aware of the fact that the Syrian *ketubbah* today *still* contains such a condition, as does the *ketubbah* in some other Sephardic communities? By the way, how come a man was allowed to marry more than one wife according to Jewish law when we are all aware of the decree of Rabbenu Gershom (who lived in the tenth century) which forbade a man from marrying more than one wife?

(Teacher passes around a facsimile of the Syrian *ketubbah*.)

Student: The Sephardic communities did not come under the jurisdiction of the decree of Rabbi Gershom, and while it was not very common, polygamy was permitted in certain Sephardic communities, especially when there were the kinds of problems that you have just described.

(The teacher should be very careful to make the girls understand that the reason for the inclusion of this clause in the *ketubbah* was in order that procreation and the continuation of the family could be achieved. In many instances in places like Morocco, where a woman was barren, she was treated with all the love, affection, and financial security and amenities that she would otherwise have received even though the husband took a second wife in order to perpetuate his family's name. While this is all "academic" in North American society, the idea behind the problem and the noble purpose of procreation should be projected as the reason for the *ketubbah's* clause so as to dispel concepts of male chauvinism and a double standard of life for husband and wife within Judaism.)

Student: Today, with so many Orthodox obstetricians and fertility experts in the medical field, many of these problems can be alleviated!

Teacher: You are very correct, and while this is not a problem that we should focus further attention on, I only brought it into this sphere of our conversation so that many of the misconceptions about the respect of husband and wife and their respective roles in Jewish society could be dispelled. As you all know, a husband is responsible by Jewish law for the tendering of affection and proper clothing and shelter and care for his wife. This is part of the obligation he undertakes in the *ketubbah*. In this connection, I would like to ask a question! Why is it that the man chooses the wife? Don't women have something to say, or at least as much to say, in the choice of a husband?

Student: I would like to respond to the question, which is an excellent one, because there are many misconceptions about this matter as well. It is well known from the Torah, the Talmud, and Halakhah, as represented in an abundance of quotations, that a girl *may not* be married or given in marriage *against her will*. Even in the olden days, when a father would contract for the marriage of his female child to the male child of someone else, she always had the right of refusal if she did not wish to accept the young man when they were both of age to make discriminatory judgments about one another.

Teacher: The fact is that the woman has to accept what is offered her for the *kinyan* (legal acquisition of a wife) at the time that her prospective husband makes this offer to her. She has the right to refuse at that time. There was further protection against women being married by force, or being carried off by men who might wish to force them into becoming their wives. It is for these reasons that a woman must be married in front of two duly qualified Jewish witnesses and that a wedding is a public ceremony which must take place in the presence of a *minyan* (a quorum of at least ten adult males). In most Sephardic communities the rabbis made a decree that no marriage that was performed without proper witnesses and a *minyan* would be accepted as a marriage. Why do you think they did so?

Student: This both provided for the need for a public occasion which gave public announcement to the fact that the man and wife were married, thereby notifying the world of the *kiddushin* and the exclusivity of their relationship as husband and wife, as well as to serve to protect women from being taken as wives by force when they would not want to submit to the overtures of an overbearing suitor.

Teacher: Today I think we have introduced a topic of major importance both for you as individuals and for the continuity of Jewish life as we want to see it. Many issues of the women's rights within Judaism have been discussed, the sanctity of marriage as a God-ordained union in which He Himself becomes a partner, the importance of procreation as the fulfillment of the primary purpose of marriage, and the selection of spouses of like interest, background, and inclination, especially as regards the preservation of Torah values, have provided us with an excellent background of ideas to think about and consider. Our next lesson will deal with the specifics of the engagement ceremonies and the marriage ceremony itself. These customs will give further support to the concepts we discussed today and to the idea and ideal of marriage as *Kiddushin,* the consecration of man and wife in the fulfillment of God's will on earth. With this summary, I bid you to consider and to review some of the biblical quotations and other halakhic sources we have discussed in preparation for our next lesson on this subject, as well as the following voluntary assignment. I would like you to interview a couple about to get married, and one that has been married for one year, to discuss the concepts and values we have spoken about today in connection with the role of marriage and Jewish family.

(The teacher asks for volunteers to conduct these interviews. Six girls respond. The others do not.)

Teacher: The homework for the rest of the class is: Read about the Syrian engagement and marriage customs as described in a recent book entitled *Magic Carpet: Aleppo-in-Flatbush: The Story of our Unique Ethnic Jewish Community* by Joseph A.D. Sutton, Foreword by S.D. Goitein, published by Thayer-Jacoby, New York. Specific references are to pages 54, 55, 56, 58, 189, 195, 196, 225. Read the *Jews of Rhodes: The History of a Sephardic Community* by Marc D. Angel, published by Sepher-Hermon Press, and the Union of Sephardic Congregations, New York, 1978, the chapter entitled: "The Role of Women," pages

89 to 101. Review *Shulḥan Arukh, Eben Haezer:* Laws of Engagement: 51-56; Dowry: 58; *Ḥuppah:* 61; *Sheba Berakhot:* 62; Laws of *Ketubbah* 66; *Yalkut Meam Loez:* The Fast of the Bride and Groom: Debarim Gimmel: 853; Custom to send Bridegroom a *Tallit:* Debarim Gimmel: 857.

Kindly complete the questions on the guide sheet after you have read these sources and hand it in next class.

Shalom! Class is adjourned!

MODEL LESSON IV

CYCLE III

SELECTION OF A MATE, ENGAGEMENT, AND MARRIAGE

Lesson II

(Second session)

(Reenactment of a class session)

Target Population

A class of senior Yeshiva high school girls.

Time

A period of fifty minutes.

OBJECTIVES

Informational and Values

1. To demonstrate through the ceremonies preparatory to marriage, such as engagement ceremonies, pre-wedding ceremonies, and the marriage ceremony itself, that although all of life in the animal kingdom, which includes the human realm, is confined by certain biological needs, drives, and limitations, that the Jewish marriage, by its very name *Kiddushin* (a holy union), emphasizes a higher purpose which declares that the destiny of man, unlike that of the animal, who simply returns to the earth, is geared to the realm of eternal life, *Olam Haba,* and that God Himself is part Matchmaker and even an Escort of the

young couple as they march down the aisle. The Almighty is also the Partner in their household Who is the third Partner in helping to bring about their progeny who will come into this world thanks to the Almighty, and the father and mother of the children.

2. To learn the elements of the marriage ceremony so as to be prepared to participate in such a ceremony in a knowledgeable manner either as a bridesmaid or preferably as a bride.
3. That the wedding and all the various preliminary ceremonies confer the utmost of significance upon marriage as the time of supreme joy and happiness in Jewish life for the couple, their respective parents, and their families and friends, as well as for *Klal Yisrael*, the entire Jewish people, whose eternity will be preserved and perpetuated by such joyous occasions which will hopefully give rise to future generations of Jews for all time to come.
4. That the description of the various ceremonies relating to the periods prior to, during, and following the marriage, will help to launch the young couple into a life of sanctity, Jewish happiness, and a fruitful and blissful union. The explanations of the various symbolic acts related to the various ceremonies will convey the importance of these observances to the student.

MATERIALS

1. A Syrian and a Moroccan *Ketubbah*
2. A plain wedding band
3. A *Tallit*
4. A glass covered by a napkin
5. Pictures of various types of Sephardic bridal gowns from Morocco and the Eastern communities

METHOD

1. The teacher made brief reference to preliminary discussion of *Lesson One*, which set the stage for the description of the actual pre-wedding ceremonies which will emphasize the notion of the holiness of marriage and the importance of

the young couple entering into marriage in a state of spiritual cleanliness and sanctity.

2. The teacher motivated students by passing around various objects relating to the ceremony of the wedding and its preliminary activities which should capture the interest and curiosity of the students.
3. The teacher determined prior level of knowledge by the questioning of the students on their homework assignment. He issued a brief guide sheet for them to complete and hand in to him.
4. The teacher added to their knowledge by providing explanations available from use of *A Treasury of Sephardic Laws and Customs*.

PRESENTATION BY TEACHER (rendered in the present tense)

Teacher: During the course of our first lesson on the topic of "Selecting a Mate, Engagement, and Marriage," we discussed many of the important issues to you which relate to the Torah perspective in seeking the kind of prospective mate whose background, interests, and destiny coincide with your own trend of thinking. Our discussion focused on the importance of the Jewish woman as the conveyor of Jewish eternity through the bearing of children who are the links in the eternal chain of Jewish life. The respect for the role of the woman, her rights and her importance, will be further delineated today as we describe the actual details of the preliminary ceremonies prior to the wedding, during the wedding, and following it. These ceremonies, in the native countries of the various Sephardic Jews, could take place over an extended period ranging from two to three weeks duration. Here in North America they also take place over many weeks. Much energy, money, and the expenditure of a great deal of effort in the preparation and much loving care goes into making this most joyous day in the lives of a young couple a day of supreme happiness and perfection for them.

When you read the suggested homework readings

which I gave you, you surely acquired a sense of the pomp and concern expressed by the Syrian and Judeo-Spanish communities for these ceremonies. In the Moroccan tradition the number of events held in advance of a wedding surpasses that of all of the other groups we have described, and this information is available in great detail in the French language in an excellent book by Professor Issachar Ben-Ami of the Hebrew University entitled *Le Judaisme Marocain: Etudes Ethno-Culturelles* published by Rubin Mass, Jerusalem, 1975. This book, which is also partially written in Hebrew, is called *Yahadut Marokko* and has many beautiful descriptions of the folklore, the Maimuna, and other expressive Moroccan traditions. However, the extensive and fascinating articles on all of the preludes and traditions relating to the Moroccan marriage are in the French language, and I will, during the course of our discussion, share some of these very beautiful traditions with you.

(The preceding introduction and description of the Moroccan traditions should be reserved for a class that is going to discuss Moroccan marriage traditions rather than the Syrian or Judeo-Spanish, or Spanish and Portuguese traditions. In such case the teacher would present the Moroccan material later in the session.)

Teacher: I assume that most of you have read the homework assignment, and I will ask for students to volunteer some information to describe the preliminary ceremonies in the Syrian community that would mark the engagement of a young couple.

Student: I was amazed to see that only a few decades ago, most of the Syrian marriages were arranged marriages made by a *shadkhan* (marriage broker) within the community who was a very highly respected and pious member of the community who would go about matching bride and groom in accordance with many of the principles that we discussed in our last class. I was also impressed by the fact that his wife also played an important role and always accompanied him so that she could both handle the sensitive matters of information that should be imparted to the prospective bride, and that he should not have to be alone when visiting widowed mothers or divorced mothers, which would violate the concept of *yiḥud*.

Student: I get the impression from what I read that a Syrian young man has to be very serious about a young woman if he dates her three times, because then he can expect to be asked about his intentions by the father of the girl after the dates have gone beyond that number. If his intentions are serious and honorable and acceptable to the prospective father-in-law, their relationship is permitted to continue for a while. But it is not very long before the boy's parents call the parents of the girl to say that they are "coming over," which formalizes the fact that the couple intend to marry and represents a very large family gathering of both sides of the couple. To me it seemed like the *kinyan* (the symbolic act of acquiring something or entering into agreement) is very much like the *tenaim* that is practiced by Ashkenazic Jews, especially those of Ḥassidic orientation. Of course, the sumptuous meal prepared by the mother of the prospective bride and her relatives and the *nobeh,* which is the orchestra playing all those special Near Eastern musical instruments, make it all sound like a very joyous and entertaining kind of occasion. One thing for sure is that the bride and groom to be are presented with an abundance of gifts by their visiting relatives.

Teacher: Do you get the impression that this is simply a social occasion? Or did you get the feeling that there was a very serious dimension of activities in preparation for the wedding at this ceremony?

Student: Oh no! The actual *kinyan* ceremony enacted immediately after the dinner is a very serious and important ceremony which will be enacted by the rabbi who will make the *kinyan* with a handkerchief from the fathers of the bride and the groom, indicating that all of the parents have agreed to the marriage. It was interesting to learn that in olden days the parents would bring along the money for the dowry for the children which the rabbi would hold in escrow. It was on that occasion that the date for the wedding would be announced, which of course formalized the forthcoming marriage in a way that fulfills the Jewish tradition of *Ein mekadeshin beli shidukhin*.

Teacher: What other important preliminary ceremonies to the wedding impressed you?

Student: The *sweheni*, which is the evening party marking the immersion in the *mikveh* (ritual bath) by the bride, who performs *tebilah* (ritual immersion) prior to the wedding, is a very beautiful occasion. All the trays or "platters" which are sent by the future bridegroom to his fiancée and the gifts that are brought by the women who come to this party should surely make this the most memorable night in a girl's life. The inclusion of a very ornate, costly handbag which has in it money to cover the cost for attending the *mikveh*, as well as the many personal gifts of fragrances, soaps, lotions, etc., which the women bring, can only help the young bride to remember her first immersion as a very special occasion. The fact that this party also is used for the bride-to-be to show her trousseau and that a small group of women accompany her to the *mikveh*, after which she will partake of delicious sweets, oriental pastries, and the sipping of a special milk made out of almonds and heavily sweetned with sugar, together with them, will surely make an indelible impression upon the young woman who will be expected to "renew herself" in spiritual cleanliness for her husband each month throughout her reproductive years.

Teacher: What is the symbolism of the three trays that are usually present at the *sweheni* (or "night of the bath party")?

Student: Some say that the custom of the three trays is to symbolically be reminiscent of the biblical quote, "And I will betroth thee unto me forever; Yea, I will betroth thee unto me in righteousness, and in judgement, and in loving kindness, and in mercy; I will even betroth thee unto me in faithfulness and thou shalt know the Lord" (Hosea 2:21-22).

I was very impressed by the fact that the *sweheni* ceremony, which is attended by all of the women in the family, takes on the air of such a public-type occasion. While it is true that most of us think of going to the *mikveh* as a very private matter (which it surely is after this first formal occasion), there is much to be said for the public attention given by all of the women to this special initiation into *taharat hamishpaḥa* (family purity): The women who join in the party and place henna (red vegetable dye) on their hand as a sign of joy and against the evil eye, in a sense join spiritually with the bride-to-be in the supreme happiness which is hers in her future as she is about to build a future Jewish home. The fact that in ancient Syria musicians accompanied the bride-to-be to the *mikveh* while she was escorted by her family, and the fact that even today as the bride-to-be emerges from the *mikveh* she is given such special delicacies in which they all share, makes public the importance of Jewish family purity in a way that has an enduring impact in the community. This surely must account for the fact that such a high percentage of the Syrian women attend the *mikveh* here in our own community.

Teacher: There are similar preliminary occasions marked by the Judeo-Spanish and the Moroccan communities, all of which have the same effect that you just mentioned, namely, to make public the importance of attending the *mikveh* and the sanctity of *taharat hamishpaḥa* as one of the cornerstones of a healthy Jewish marriage. I am glad to see that you have done your reading and that you have found it of interest. Now, please tell me about some of the differences in custom!

Student: The actual wedding ceremony itself is different from the Ashkenazic ceremony in several respects. One is that *three* blessings are recited under *Birkat Erusin,* the same two blessings over the wine and *erusin,* with the addition of the blessing *Bore minei besamim* over spices. That makes *three* blessings instead of only *two* in the beginning of the ceremony. There are also other differences in the Sephardic tradition that I will leave for someone else to describe! I refer to the *ketubbah,* in particular!

Student: Well, I see that the Sephardic *ketubbah* is not read at a Syrian wedding! When is it prepared and how is it properly documented and witnessed if it is not done in a public manner?

Teacher: The *ketubbah* is properly signed by two duly qualified witnesses prior to the wedding ceremony. However, a *kinyan* is again made under the *ḥuppah,* where the bride receives from the *ḥatan* the *ketubbah,* which she is always to keep. What else did you notice that is different?

Student: Well, I was surprised to learn that the veiling of the bride was not really for the purpose that I had always thought. It was always my understanding that the veiling of the bride was to teach that "beauty is only skin deep" and that the beauty that comes from within is the only beauty that counts in Jewish life. However, I understand that the Syrian custom is to be *bodek et hakallah* (to investigate that the woman is the proper one who will be married by the *ḥatan)* and not the *badeken kallah* (to cover or veil the bride) which the Ashkenazim do!

Teacher: Yes, this is in fulfillment of a Halakhah that "a man is forbidden to marry a woman until he sees her." What else is different in regard to the actual betrothal?

Student: I was especially surprised to see that besides the fact that the *ketubbah* is not read, the *ḥatan* gives the girl an actual *silver coin* instead of a *ring* at first and that his proclamation is to her, "I betroth thee to me with this silver coin" *(bekaspa hadein)!*

Teacher: Yes, this is in fulfillment of the rabbinic teaching of the Talmud that one of the three ways in which a woman is acquired for marriage is through *kesef* (a silver coin), and therefore the ceremony follows this tradition. A ring is also good because *shaveh kesef kekesef* (an object of the value of silver is the equivalent of the silver). The girl gets a ring immediately afterwards. I would also like to point out that actually the original reason for reading the *Ketubbah* was really to distinguish between the *Erusin* (betrothal) and the *Nesuin* (or *Kiddushin),* the actual marriage. Thus the reading of the *Ketubbah* was to divide between these two portions of the wedding ceremony which today we perform together but which were enacted separately in earlier times. Also the Syrian *Ketubbah* includes a lot of numbers five and eighteen, which is in keeping with their tradition that the number five is a good luck omen, as derived from *Ben porat Yosef ben porat* (five words) which refers to the biblical quotation in Genesis 49:22, "Joseph is a fruitful vine, a fruitful vine by a fountain; its branches run over the wall." And as you know the tradition relates the concept that Joseph was freed from the evil eye. This therefore confers the full blessing of the community upon the young couple in a way that protects against the evil eye, which has always been a matter of concern in the Eastern communities, in particular.

(The teacher passes around a Syrian and a Moroccan *ketubbah* for the students to read [which is in Aramaic]. The teacher will make reference to the significant portions of the *ketubbah* and translates them to be sure that the class understands the items under discussion.)

Teacher: What other special difference did you notice in the *ḥuppah?*

Student: I noticed that the *ḥuppah* was made by spreading a *tallit* over the heads of the bride and groom by their respective fathers. I also read that the groom received his *tallit* from his bride as a gift, and since it is a new one, he makes the *Sheheḥeyanu* prayer and that this *tallit* is used while the *Sheba Berakhot* are recited under the *ḥuppah.*

Student: I also noticed that the last of the *Sheba Berakhot* ends with the words *Umaẓliaḥ,* which is different.

Student: I heard that *yiḥud* (the isolation of bride and groom after the marriage ceremony) does not always take place at a Syrian *ḥuppah*, and that it does not always take place at a Moroccan *ḥuppah* either! Is that true?

Teacher: Yes, it is! Because some regard the actual *ḥuppah* as being done under a *tallit*, which demonstrates a form of *yiḥud*. Also, it is considered by the Syrians that the *Seudat miẓvah* (banquet) which follows the wedding ceremony and the continued *Sheba Berakhot* (seven benedictions) which are recited at the conclusion of the wedding banquet do not constitute an interruption in the service, so that the actual *yiḥud* takes place when the bride and groom retire to their privacy after the whole wedding celebration is concluded. However, in some Syrian communities there is *yiḥud*, and it is observed for twelve minutes.

Student: It was especially interesting to read that on the Sabbath prior to the wedding, which is similar to the Ashkenazic *Aufruf* (when the bridegroom is called to the Torah), that this special Syrian ceremony named *Arus* (for the one who is to get married) confers added special recognition upon the bridegroom by the singing of special *piyutim*. Also on the Sabbath *after* his wedding or when he has returned from his honeymoon, the *Abraham Siv*, which is the reading of the portion from the Bible about Abraham which is translated into the Aramaic, again confers special recognition upon the bridegroom. This surely makes the *ḥatan* an important part of the community from the inception of his marriage, and that should go a long way in keeping him as an active member in the congregation!

Teacher: As you know, not all Syrians observe the full week of *Sheba Berakhot*, since these ceremonies which were observed in Aleppo were interrupted when they made their way to America. However, those Syrian Jews who come from Damascus do observe the complete week of *Sheba Berakhot*, and as a result the wedding honeymoon is always postponed among the Damascenes. Here is an interesting question to ponder.

What happens when there is an intramarriage between a Sephardi and an Ashkenaziah?

(Several wrong answers are offered by the students. The teacher then continues.)

Teacher: The wife follows the tradition of the husband in all cases and will therefore (with the permission of her parents) follow all of his traditions and bring up a Syrian Jewish family. In the case of a Syrian girl marrying an Ashkenazic boy, the opposite would be true. Many of those traditions showing what the procedures are in order to accommodate the respective families of groom and bride will be described in future lessons when we discuss the special honors that are given out at the *Berit Milah* when, please God, the fruitful marriage brings forth a male child, and at the *Pidyon Haben,* etc., or how these honors are accorded at the *Zebed Habat,* the ceremony for naming a girl.

I would like to draw your attention to the fact that the custom of fasting on the day of the wedding was observed in Syria, but does not seem to be practiced here today. Who knows why?

Student: Fasting on the day of the wedding by the bride and groom is observed by some Sephardic Jews and not by others. Some feel that the reason for fasting (and reciting the special *Amidah* for *Minḥa* with the *Vidui* of *Ereb Yom Kippur)* is enacted so that the bride and groom will enter marriage forgiven for all their sins. Others say the reason for fasting is to be certain that the bride and groom do not become intoxicated prior to the *ḥuppah.* Therefore, even those who do not fast are certain not to partake of liquor before the wedding ceremony.

Summary by Teacher

I think that we can conclude our lesson by first recognizing the great beauty that exists within the tradition. One point that was not mentioned, which is of course part of every Jewish wedding ceremony, is the remembrance of the destruction of the Holy Temple which the Sephardic Jews enact by the recitation of "If I forget thee, O Jerusalem," etc.

I conclude by reminding you that it is precisely because of the destruction of the Temple (the *Bet Hamikdash)* that the rebuilding of every Jewish home by the observance of Halakhah and the sanctity of Jewish life which has kept our Torah alive even in times when the Holy Temple itself has been destroyed, is the answer to the challenges to the survival of our Jewish people. We have survived even though we were sometimes out of our own land, and for the last 2,000 years we were without our Holy Temple. We believe we have survived to this day because brides and grooms have made their Jewish homes a "minor sanctuary" in which there was always room for God. I hope that I shall be privileged to attend many of your weddings in the not too distant future, weddings that will reflect the same kinds of high standards that we have discussed.

Now that we have studied about the laws and customs of marriage regarding to the Sephardic tradition, I am pleased to announce that the rabbi of the local Syrian synagogue has invited our class to witness a Syrian Jewish wedding in his congregation within the next few weeks. We will have ample advance notice so that we can all dress up for that occasion.

Please hand in your guide sheets that you had for homework.

Before we adjourn, I would like us to spend the next ten minutes listening to a few of the reports on the interviews some of you volunteered to do with young couples about to marry and with couples married for one year.

(These students report on their interview — two with young couples about to get married and one with a couple that has been married for one year. There is a great deal of interest shown by the class.)

Teacher: The homework assignment for everyone else is to write one page of their reaction to the responses given by the interviewees. These are to be handed in at our next session.

Shalom!

Class is adjourned.

Early Childhood

PART 1 — CHAPTER 1

Basic Sources

For an overview of the Halakhah relating to the topics covered in this unit, it is suggested that the teacher review the following basic sources which can be distributed as advance assignments to students.

1. *Shulḥan Arukh, Yoreh Deah* — Laws of *Milah*

   Law of Father Circumcising His Own Son: 261
   Laws of Circumcision: 262, 264
   Order of Circumcision Service: 265
   Laws of Redemption of First-Born: 305

2. *Mekor Ḥayyim Hashalem,* Vol. V

   Laws of *Milah:* 248
   Laws of Redemption of First-Born: 249
   Laws of Naming a Child: 251

3. *Meam Loez*

   Customs for Naming a Child: Bereshit Bet: 685
   Laws of *Milah:* Bereshit Alef: 327
   Order of *Berit Milah* Service: Bereshit Alef: 334, 335
   Elijah the Prophet at the *Berit Milah:* Debarim Alef: 34
   The Importance of *Milah:* Shemot Alef: 64
   Kaddish at *Milah:* Bereshit Alef: 337
   Mohel: Bereshit Alef: 332–334
   Laws of Redemption of First-Born: Shemot Alef: 222–224
   Shemot Alef: 221
   Raising an Orphan: Shemot Bet: 801

Questions for Class Review or Homework Assignments

1. How do Sephardim differ from Ashkenazim in customs of naming children? Are there any exceptions among Sephardim?

2. Describe a distinctive custom in your own community relating to naming a child.
3. What difference is there in the kind(s) of precircumcision special gatherings held by Sephardim and Ashkenazim?
4. What is the relationship of Lilith to the precircumcision customs?
5. Name the participants in the *Berit Milah* ceremonies and describe their respective roles.
6. Does the *Kohen* keep the silver coins from the *Pidyon Haben*? What is the halakhic basis for this?
7. Describe a unique custom in your community relating to the *Pidyon Haben*.

Topics for Class Discussion

1. Some communities allow a *Berit Milah* to take place in the afternoon in order to accommodate the crowd. Discuss the halakhic implications and the opposing viewpoints. (See *Yabia Omer,* vol. 2: *Eben Haezer* 18.)
2. What are the halakhic considerations which support the preference for the adoption of either a Jewish child or a non-Jewish child?
3. Discuss the possible approaches to the problem of having two *baalei berit* in a synagogue at the same time on a Monday or Thursday as regards the distribution of *aliyot* to the Torah. (See *Yabia Omer,* vol. 6, *Oraḥ Ḥayyim* 23.)
4. Describe the different ways in which the problem of *safek kehunah* (uncertainty of the Priesthood) can be avoided in connection with the presenting of the five silver *shekalim*.
5. How should one handle the custom to name for the living when the mother of the child is of Ashkenazic background?
6. Discuss the concept of *shiluv,* which represents the Kabbalistic view that the soul of man is interwoven with the name given to him.

Bar Miẓvah

PART 1 — CHAPTER 2

Basic Sources

For an overview of the Halakhah relating to the topics covered in this unit, it is suggested that the teacher review the following basic sources which can be distributed as advance assignments to students.

1. *Shulḥan Arukh, Oraḥ Ḥayyim*

   Magen Abraham: 225:4

2. *Mekor Ḥayyim Hashalem*

   Vol. 1, Status of Bar Miẓvah: 152
   Vol. 2, 188–191
   Girl Becomes of Majority Age at Twelve Years: 190
   Introduction about Bar Miẓvah: 188

3. *Ben Ish Ḥay* — The Recitation of the *Sheheḥeyanu* by the Bar Miẓvah Boy, Shana Rishona, Parashat Re'eh

4. *Meam Loez*

   Bar Miẓvah During Month of Adar: Bereshit Alef: 64

Questions for Class Review or Homework Assignments

1. At what age does a boy begin to train to put on *tefillin* in the tradition to which you are accustomed? What is the halakhic reason to support this practice?
2. Describe the special ceremonies which are enacted on the day the lad puts on *tefillin* for the first time according to your tradition.

3. Which *aliyah* is accorded to the Bar Miẓvah boy on the Shabbat he is called to the Torah according to the customs of two different Sephardic communities?
4. How do Sephardim differ from Ashkenazim in the recitation of the blessings over the *tefillin*?
5. Why do some men wear two pairs of *tefillin,* and when do they put them on?
6. What form of celebration is held for family and friends to mark the Bar Miẓvah?

Topics for Class Discussion

1. Discuss the halakhic issues involved in whether or not the father should recite the blessings over the Torah with the boy who is called to the Torah on a Monday or Thursday when he puts on his *tefillin* for the first time while he is younger than thirteen years of age.
2. What are the considerations behind the fact that Sephardim do not recite the *Barukh sheptarani* when the Bar Miẓvah boy is called to the Torah when he is thirteen years of age?
3. Since the *drush* or *drasha* of the Bar Miẓvah has always been such a traditional part of the occasion, how do you account for the fact that some Sephardim no longer have this dissertation by the Bar Miẓvah boy as part of the ceremonies?
4. How do you feel about the lavish manner in which some celebrate the Bar Miẓvah nowadays? Does the occasion warrant the tremendous outlay of finance, energy, and time? How does one who is not affluent celebrate in a meaningful way? Are there possible alternatives to the current types of celebrations which could capture the essence and spirit of the Bar Miẓvah and perhaps serve a more meaningful purpose?
5. When does a girl assume responsibility for observing the *miẓvot*? What are the *miẓvot* for which she is responsible, and from which is she free?

Engagement and Marriage
PART 1 — CHAPTER 3

Basic Sources

For an overview of the Halakhah relating to the topics covered in this unit, it is suggested that the teacher review the following basic sources which can be distributed as advance assignments to students.

1. *Shulḥan Arukh, Eben Haezer*

    Laws of Engagement: 51–56
    Dowry: 58
    Ḥuppah: 61
    Sheba Berakhot: 62
    Laws of the *Ketubbah:* 66

2. *Mekor Ḥayyim Hashalem,* vol. V

    Times Forbidden to Hold a Wedding, Laws of the *Kallah* and Her State of Purity to Enter a *Ḥuppah,* The Sabbath Before the Wedding, and the Wedding Day Fast: 236
    Laws of the *Ketubbah:* 237
    Laws of the *Ḥuppah:* 237
    Wearing a *Tallit* at the *Ḥuppah,* Blessings and Laws of *Erusin* and *Kiddushin,* Blessings of Marriage and the Breaking of the Glass: 237
    Laws of *Sheba Berakhot,* The Sabbath After the Wedding: 238

3. *Ben Ish Ḥay,* Laws of Marriage, Shana Rishona, Parashat Shoftim

4. *Yalkut Meam Loez*

    Blessings of *Erusin:* Debarim Gimmel: 852

Laws of Marriage: Bereshit Bet: 575, 502, 508, 483; Bereshit Alef: 92
Laws of the Bridegroom and Bride: Bereshit Bet: 575
The Fast of the Bride and Groom: Debarim Gimmel: 853
Custom to Send Bridegroom a *Tallit:* Debarim Gimmel: 857
Customs of *Ḥuppah:* Debarim Gimmel: 853

Questions for Class Review or Homework Assignments

1. What is the form of formal agreement which marks the engagement of a couple about to marry in your community? Is there a special gathering to mark this ceremony? If so, who are the principal participants?
2. Describe the ceremonies relating to the celebration marking the evening of "the bride's bath" in your community. Why is this occasion deemed to be so important?
3. Do you have the tradition to veil the bride? Why?
4. In what way are the Sephardic *Birkat Erusin* different from those of the Ashkenazim?
5. Do you read the *ketubbah* during the wedding ceremony in your tradition, and, if not, when is this important feature of the wedding procedure enacted?
6. What does the groom give to his bride under the *ḥuppah* to effectuate the marriage?
7. What role does the *tallit* play in the wedding ceremony of your community?
8. Describe the ceremonies in the synagogue in connection with the bridegroom on the Sabbath before the wedding, or the Sabbath after the wedding, or both Sabbaths, if something special relates to the bridegroom on these Sabbaths.

Topics for Class Discussion

1. How do you feel about the concept of the *shadkhan* and arranged marriages?

2. What is the Jewish legal status of the bride and groom after the formal engagement ceremony, such as a *kinyan*? What happens if they wish to break the engagement?
3. Describe and discuss the differences in the Sephardic *ketubbah* and its implications as regards a woman who is barren after ten years. What was the tradition of polygamy in the native country of your particular community? Has this affected the attitude towards a wife by the Sephardic husband?
4. Why do some Sephardim not require *yiḥud*? On what halakhic basis can this custom be understood?
5. Discuss the times that weddings may not take place in your community and explain the rationale for these practices.
6. How does a family, where there is an intramarriage between Sephardic and Ashkenazic spouses, abide by Jewish tradition? Who follows whom, and in what areas can there be a compromise?

Divorce and Ḥaliẓah

PART 1 — CHAPTER 4

Basic Sources

For an overview of the Halakhah relating to the topics covered in this unit, it is suggested that the teacher review the following basic sources which can be distributed as advance assignments to students.

1. *Shulḥan Arukh, Eben Haezer*

    Laws of *Gittin:* 119
    Names of the Husband and Wife in the Divorce: 129
    Laws of *Yibum:* 156
    Laws of Ḥaliẓah: 169–177

2. *Mekor Ḥayyim Hashalem*, Vol. V

    Divorce: 247

3. *Meam Loez*

    Laws of When It Is Permissible to Divorce: Debarim Gimmel: 907
    Laws of Divorce: Debarim Gimmel: 909–917
    Text of the Divorce: Debarim Gimmel: 911

Questions for Class Review or Homework Assignment

1. What are the general grounds for divorce today?
2. How does one arrange for a bona fide religious divorce *(get)* which will be valid so that the individuals who are separating may marry someone else?
3. How long must a divorcee wait before remarrying and why?

4. Whom may a divorcee not marry?
5. Who are the main participants in the divorce proceedings, other than the husband and wife about to divorce? Describe the role of each of them.
6. Who are all the participants in the *ḥaliẓah* ceremony?

Topics for Class Discussion

1. What is the attitude towards divorce in your community? Are there many divorces? What can be done to prevent divorces in the community?
2. Discuss the anomaly that, in the Eastern communities from which most of Israel's Sephardim originate, a man could grant his wife a divorce with relative ease and yet there was relatively little divorce among them.
3. Do you think that a Torah way of life preserves marital harmony and mutual respect in marriage? Explain why.
4. What are the halakhic considerations in either permitting *yibum* or prohibiting it today?

Death, Burial, Mourning and Memorial Observances

PART 1 — CHAPTER 5

Basic Sources

For an overview of the Halakhah relating to the topics covered in this unit, it is suggested that the teacher review the following basic sources which can be distributed as advance assignments to students.

1. *Shulḥan Arukh, Yoreh Deah*

   Laws of the Sick: 335
   Laws of *Vidui:* 338
   Laws of *Keriah:* 340
   Laws of Attending a Funeral: 343
   Obligations to Bury the Dead: 362
   The Period of Mourning: 375
   Comforting the Mourners: 376
   Laws of Mourner's Meal: 378
   Things Forbidden to a Mourner: 380, 391
   Laws of the Seven Days of Mourning: 393
   Laws of Mourning on the Sabbath: 400

2. *Mekor Ḥayyim Hashalem,* Vol. V

   Sickness and Laws of Visiting the Sick: 278
   Expiration of the Soul: 279
   Laws of *Keriah:* 280
   Escorting the Dead to the Grave and *Hesped:* 282, 283
   Laws of Mourning, Meal of Condolence, and Comforting Mourners: 285
   Laws of the Seven Days of Mourning: 286
   Laws of the Thirty Days of Mourning: 287
   Laws of Mourning on Festivals and Holidays: 288
   Customs Performed to Benefit the Soul of the Deceased: 290

Laws of *Kaddish:* 291
Laws of *Maftir* and *Hashkabah:* 292
The *Yahrẓeit:* 293
Laws of Visiting the Cemetery: 294
Laws of the Graves of Parents and *Ẓaddikim:* 295

3. *Kiẓur Shulḥan Arukh Hashalem,* Vol. 1

Laws of the Mourner and Those Who Occupy Themselves With Tending the Dead Are Exempt from *Shema:* 14

2. *Yalkut Meam Loez*

Laws of Visiting the Sick: Bereshit Alef: 345
Laws of Burial: Bereshit Bet: 826
Laws of Mourning: Bereshit Bet: 823
Seven Days of Mourning: Bereshit Bet: 502, 828
Meal of Condolence: Bereshit Bet: 521
Hesped: Bereshit Bet: 463; Vayikra: 107
Kaddish: Bereshit Alef: 367; 210, 373

Questions for Class Review or Homework Assignment

1. What are the duties of the Ḥebra Kaddisha? Does your community have its own Ḥebra Kaddisha? If not, who handles this important responsibility for the community?
2. Describe the basic procedure at a funeral in your community.
3. Who among the mourners do not go to the cemetery for a father?
4. What is the general custom regarding women going to the cemetery?
5. Where is the special *Kaddish* after the burial service recited?
6. When is *keriah* enacted in your community?
7. Describe the mourners' meal. Who provides this for the mourners?
8. Describe the basic observances of *Shibah,* including those

of religious services held in the house of mourning, special prayers in the *Shibah* house, etc.

9. What special ceremonies take place in the synagogue on the Sabbath during *Shibah*?
10. Describe the ceremony concluding the *Shibah* according to the custom of your community.
11. Name and describe the occasions when they conduct a study session in memory of the deceased throughout the "year" of mourning for a parent.
12. Name all the occasions when *Hashkabah* is said during the "year" of mourning.
13. Describe fully the observance of the annual *Yahrẓeit* including personal conduct, home, and synagogue traditions. What does your community call this annual observance?
14. What are the times of the year when one goes to visit the grave and to offer prayers there?

Topics for Class Discussion

1. Discuss the importance of maintaining a Ḥebra Kaddisha. Indicate the need for young people to recognize the importance of this great *miẓvah* which is known as *Ḥesed shel emet* so that when they become active members of the adult community, they might consider joining the men's division or women's division of the Ḥebra.
2. Discuss why such dignity and reverence is accorded the deceased during the *reḥiẓah* and the preparation for burial. Compare this with the almost barbaric practices of other cultures.
3. Discuss proper conduct for those who make a condolence call to the house of mourning.
4. Discuss the problem of autopsies and under what circumstances they could be performed.
5. Discuss and define the restrictions on a mourner for a parent for the "year" of mourning.

Symbols of the Covenant

PART II — CHAPTER 6

Basic Sources

For an overview of the Halakhah relating to the topics covered in this unit, it is suggested that the teacher review the following basic sources which can be distributed as advance assignments to students.

1. a. *Shulḥan Arukh, Oraḥ Ḥayyim*

   Laws of the Blessing for *Ẓiẓit:* 8
   Laws of the Fringes: 11
   Size of the *Tallit:* 16
   Laws of Putting On *Tallit* for First Time: 22
   Laws of Putting On *Tefillin:* 25–28
   Order of Writing *Tefillin:* 32
   Order of *Parshiot* in *Tefillin:* 34
   Time for Putting On *Tefillin:* 37

   b. *Shulḥan Arukh, Yoreh Deah*

   Laws of *Mezuzah:* 285–291

2. *Kaf Haḥayyim* — Same chapters as in *Shulḥan Arukh,* listed above

3. *Mekor Hayyim Hashalem,* Vol. I

   Introduction to Laws on *Ẓiẓit:* 19
   Fringes of *Ẓiẓit:* 23, 25
   Laws of *Tallit Katan:* 26
   Order of Putting On *Tallit:* 28
   Introduction to Laws on *Tefillin:* 29
   Order of Putting On *Tefillin* and Its Blessing: 30

Placement of *Tefillin:* 31
Time for Putting On *Tefillin:* 33
Taking Off *Tefillin:* 36
Laws of *Mezuzah:* Vol. 5, 258

4. *Kiẓur Shulḥan Arukh Hashalem,* Vol. I

Laws of *Ẓiẓit:* 9
Laws of Size of *Tallit Katan* and *Tallit Gadol:* 9
Laws Relating to the Commandment of *Tefillin:* 10

5. *Ben Ish Ḥay*

Laws of *Ẓiẓit:* Shana Rishona, Parashat Noaḥ
Making of *Ẓiẓit;* Size of *Tallit* and Time for Wearing *Ẓiẓit:* Parashat Lekh Lekha
Laws of Blessing on *Tallit:* Parashat Bereshit
Laws of *Tefillin:* Parashiot Vayera and Ḥayei Sarah
Laws of *Mezuzah:* Shana Shenia, Ki Tabo

6. *Yalkut Meam Loez*

Laws of *Ẓiẓit;* Bamidbar: 185
Blessing of *Ẓiẓit:* Bereshit Alef: 115; Bamidbar: 190
Size of *Tallit:* Bamidbar: 189
Tallit Katan: Bereshit Alef: 114
Laws of Putting On *Tefillin:* Shemot Gimmel: 1023, Debarim Bet 556
Laws of Removing *Tefillin:* Debarim Bet: 563
Laws of Inspecting *Tefillin:* Debarim Bet: 564
Laws of Installing a *Mezuzah* and Its Blessing: Debarim Bet: 581
Laws of *Mezuzah:* Debarim Bet: 580

Questions for Class Review or Homework Assignment

1. Describe how many *berakhot* are recited over the *tefillin.*
2. Are the *tefillin* put on while standing or sitting? Explain.
3. At what juncture in the Morning Service do you put on *tefillin*?

4. What differences are there between the Sephardim and Ashkenazim as relates to putting on *tefillin* on certain special days during the year?
5. What *berakha* do you recite on putting up a *mezuzah*?
6. Describe the method of making *ẓiẓit* in your community.
7. Can you describe the method of any other community as relates to making *ẓiẓit?*
8. When are the *ẓiẓit* kissed during the prayer service?

Topics for Class Discussion

1. Discuss the difference between *Rashi Tefillin* and *Rabbenu Tam Tefillin.*
2. Discuss why only very few put on two pairs of *tefillin* at the same time.
3. What is the reason for covering the head with a *tallit,* and who normally does so?
4. What is the difference between the blessings *Al miẓvat ẓiẓit* and *Lehitatef beẓiẓit*?
5. Discuss the halakhic need to wear a *tallit katan.*

Dietary Laws

PART II — CHAPTER 7

Basic Sources

For an overview of the Halakhah relating to the topics covered in this unit, it is suggested that the teacher review the following basic sources which can be distributed as advance assignments to students.

1. *Shulḥan Arukh, Yoreh Deah*

    Laws of Salting Meats: 69, 70, 73
    Laws of Milk and Cheese: 115
    Laws of Meat and Milk: 87–89
    Laws of *Stam Yeinam:* 123
    Laws of Kashering Utensils: 120
    Laws of *Ḥallah:* 322–324, 327, 329

2. *Kaf Ḥahayyim* — Same chapters as in *Shulḥan Arukh,* listed above (except for laws of *ḥallah*)

3. *Mekor Ḥayyim Hashalem,* Vol. V

    Laws of Salting Meat: 261
    Laws of Meat and Milk: 262
    Laws of Milk and Cheese: 263
    Laws of *Stam Yeinam:* 263
    Laws of Kashering Utensils: 263
    Laws of *Ḥallah:* 271

4. *Kiẓur Shulḥan Arukh Hashalem,* Vol. I

    Laws of *Ḥallah:* 41
    Laws of Salting Meat: 42

Laws of Immersion of Utensils: 43
Laws of Milk, Cheese, and Bread of a Non-Jew: 44

5. *Ben Ish Ḥay* — Shana Shenia

Laws of *Ḥallah:* Parashat Shemini
Laws of Meat: Parashat Tazria
Laws of Salting Meat: Parashat Aḥarei Mot and Parashat Kedoshim
Laws of Milk and Cheese: Parashat Emor
Laws of Meat and Milk: Parashat Behaalotekha and Parashat Shelaḥ Lekha
Laws of *Stam Yeinam:* Parashat Balak
Laws of Immersion of Utensils: Parashat Matot

6. *Yalkut Meam Loez*

Laws of *Ḥallah*: Bamidbar: 173
Laws of Salting Meat: Vayikra: 73–81
Laws of Milk: Vayikra: 123
Laws of Milk and Meat: Shemot Bet: 885–907; Debarim Bet: 647
Laws of Kashering Utensils: Bamidbar: 373; Shemot Alef: 180–184

Questions for Review or Homework Assignment

1. What is the difference between glatt kasher and other kinds of kasher meat? Which should Sephardim prefer and why?
2. When is the only occasion that dairy bread is permitted during the year?
3. What is the source and the rationale for the number of hours your community waits between meat and milk?
4. Specify one law relating to kashering utensils in which the Sephardim are more lenient than Ashkenazim.
5. Indicate some type(s) of food eaten in your community or forbidden in your community which differ(s) from others.

Topics for Class Discussion

1. Discuss the problem of saying *Kiddush* over *yayin mebushal*.
2. Discuss the different approach that some Sephardic rabbis take to the problem of meat not washed in three days, and explain under what circumstances they would be more lenient.
3. Compare the difference in the customs which relate to using a dishwasher for meat and dairy as they relate to Sephardim and Ashkenazim.
4. Discuss the problems of eating away from home on a faraway trip and how one does so within the framework of Halakhah.

Family Life

PART II — CHAPTER 8

Basic Sources

For an overview of the Halakhah relating to the topics covered in this unit, it is suggested that the teacher review the following basic sources which can be distributed as advance assignments to students.

1. *Shulḥan Arukh, Yoreh Deah*

   Honor to Parents: 240

2. *Mekor Ḥayyim Hashalem,* Vol. V

   Honor to Parents: 251
   Education of Children: 250
   Husband and Wife Relationships: 239, 240
   Modesty: 239

3. *Ben Ish Ḥay*

   Laws of Honor to Parents and Family: Shana Shenia, Shoftim
   Education of Children: Shana Shenia, Parashat Ki Teẓe

4. *Yalkut Meam Loez*

   Honor to Parents: Shemot Bet: 638; Debarim Alef: 356; Vayikra: 196
   Education of Children: Bereshit Bet: 629; Shemot Bet: 533; Debarim Gimmel: 807; Debarim Alef: 236, 239; Debarim Dalet: 1263, 1267, 1356; Shemot Gimmel: 961–962; Debarim Bet: 566–577

Husband-Wife Relationships: Bereshit Alef: 322; Debarim Gimmel: 905–906
Modesty: Bereshit Alef: 108, 205, 237, 238; Debarim Alef: 58; Shemot Gimmel: 1243–1244; Bereshit Bet: 611–612

Questions for Class Review or Homework Assignment

1. Describe the customs in your community which demonstrate honor to grandparents, parents, and older relatives.
2. How does a husband show respect for his wife?
3. What are the customs in your community regarding a married woman covering her hair?
4. What are a parent's obligations in the education of children? Is this the same for sons and daughters?

Topics for Class Discussion

1. Explain the basic changes in modern Sephardic life which caused the tremendous increase in Jewish education for girls.
2. Contrast the deep-rooted family closeness which appertained in the "Old Country" communities of most Sephardic Jews from North Africa, the Middle East, and the Balkan communities, and the characteristics of the new life some of their children have made for themselves in North America and Israel.
3. Discuss the need for modesty in dress and demeanor to which both men and women of current times should give more consideration.
4. Has the Sephardic community really preserved the filial devotion of *kibbud ab* and *kibbud em* for which it has always been known?

Communal Life and Israel

PART II — CHAPTER 9

Basic Sources

For an overview of the Halakhah relating to the topics covered in this unit, it is suggested that the teacher review the following basic sources which can be distributed as advance assignments to students.

1. *Shulḥan Arukh, Yoreh Deah*

   Laws of Respect to Scholars and Teachers: 242–244
   Laws of Talmud Torah: 246
   Laws of Charity: 247–259
   Laws of Proselytes: 268

2. *Mekor Ḥayyim Hashalem*

   Laws of Respect to Scholars and Teachers: 253
   Laws of Talmud Torah: 252
   Laws of Charity: 254
   Laws of Distributing and Collecting Charity: 255, 256
   Holiness of the Land: 266
   Laws of Forbidden Mixtures: 267
   Laws of *Orla* and *Revii:* 268
   Laws of *Terumot* and *Maaserot:* 270
   Laws of *Shemitah:* 272–276

3. *Ben Ish Ḥay* — Laws of Respect to Scholars and Teachers: Shana Shenia, Ki Teẓe.

4. *Yalkut Meam Loez*

   Laws of Respect to Scholars and Teachers: Debarim Bet: 570; Shemot Bet: 533
   Laws of Talmud Torah: Debarim Bet: 565, 572, 589
   Laws of Charity: Bereshit Bet: 516; Shemot Gimmel: 1229;

Debarim Bet: 461, 462; Shemot Gimmel: 933, 934; Bamidbar: 407; Debarim Gimmel: 945; Debarim Dalet: 1389; Debarim Gimmel: 935; Bamidbar: 31, 32; Debarim Bet: 662–673; Shemot Bet: 446; Bereshit Alef: 338; 339
Laws of Proselytes: Bereshit Bet: 654; Shemot Alef: 244; Shemot Bet: 798–799; Shemot Bet: 869; Bamidbar: 35; Debarim Bet: 521; Debarim Gimmel: 1010; Shemot Bet: 439
Settlement of the Land: Bereshit Bet: 553
Boundries: Shemot Bet: 915; Debarim Bet: 593
In Praise of the Land and Its Inhabitants: Debarim Alef: 204; Debarim Alef: 194; Debarim Dalet: 1325; Bamidbar: 155; Debarim Bet: 525, 438; 411; Bereshit Bet: 477

Questions for Class Review or Homework Assignment

1. What are the traditional organizations within the local Jewish community which serve the basic needs of its members?
2. Describe the functions of a Bet Din.
3. How does the community secure the necessary funds to support its Jewish communal agencies? How was it done in the days of the *Mishkan* and the First and Second Commonwealths?
4. What are some of the institutions in the Jewish community which have almost disappeared due to neglect in our times?
5. What is the Jewish community's attitude toward accepting proselytes?
6. How does the Jewish community regard apostates?
7. Describe how *ẓedakah* is enacted in daily life to support the local and international causes of our people.
8. Who were the real pioneers of Zionism?
9. What is the current Sephardic view on *aliyah*?
10. How has North American Sephardic Jewry shown support for the Holy Land throughout the years?

11. What religious observances in the synagogue demonstrate a vital interest in the State of Israel?

Topics for Class Discussion

1. Is the concept of *Kol Yisrael arebim zeh lazeh* an operational idea within the Sephardic community of North America? If so, describe how the various communities show their common concern for the welfare of one another.
2. Is it true that the Sephardic community seeks to operate on an independent basis in providing for its Jewish communal needs? If so, is this a healthy approach? Are there alternative avenues of mutual help which should be pursued for the greater good of all?
3. List and discuss Jewish national organizations of Sephardic interest which exist and enjoy the support of all Sephardic groups.
4. Where will the Sephardic community best develop its future local and national leadership among its men and women?
5. What is the prognosis for the Sephardim in America in the next century, since they have the double problem as a "minority within a minority"?
6. Discuss the role of Sephardic Jews in the support of UJA, State of Israel Bonds, and Israeli institutions.
7. Compare the World Sephardi Federation with other international Zionist bodies. How does the World Sephardi Federation differ in its essential mission?
8. What is the best solution to the problems of the disadvantaged Israelis?
9. How can North American Sephardi and Ashkenazi students best identify with the needs of Israeli Jews?
10. Do you think that a majority of Sephardim view Israel as a primary concern? State why.

Synagogue Practices, Prayers, and Blessings

PART III — CHAPTER 10

Basic Sources

For an overview of the Halakhah relating to the topics covered in this unit, it is suggested that the teacher review the following basic sources which can be distributed as advance assignments to students.

1. a. *Shulḥan Arukh, Oraḥ Ḥayyim*

   Morning Blessing: 46, 47
   Laws of Morning Service: 48, 57
   Laws of *Keriat Shema:* 58–62
   Laws of *Nesiyat Kapayim:* 128–130
   Laws of *Taḥanunim:* 131, 134
   Laws of Reading the Torah and Related Observances: 135–149
   Laws of the Synagogue and Its Ritual Appurtenances: 154
   Laws of *Birkat Hamazon:* 182–201
   Laws of *Minḥa:* 232–234
   Laws of Arbit: 235–237

   b. *Shulḥan Arukh, Yoreh Deah*

   Laws of Writing a Torah: 270–284

2. *Kaf Haḥayyim* — Same chapters as in *Shulḥan Arukh, Oraḥ Ḥayyim*, listed above.

3. *Mekor Ḥayyim Hashalem*, Vol. I

   Laws of the Morning Blessing: 13, 14
   Laws of Sanctity of the Synagogue and Proper Conduct

in the Synagogue: 18
Laws of Morning Service: 46
Laws of *Keriat Shema:* 47, 51
Laws of *Shemoneh Esre:* 58
Repetition of the *Shemoneh Esre:* 60
Nesiyat Kapayim: 62
Laws of *Taḥanunim:* 63
Laws of *Minḥa:* 65
Laws of *Arbit:* 66, 67
Laws of *Birkat Hamazon:* Vol. II, 79–81

4. *Kiẓur Shulḥan Arukh Hashalem*

Laws of Prayer: 15
Laws of Reading the Torah: 16–19
Laws of the Torah and Its Care: 34
Laws of Conduct in the Synagogue: 15, 27
Laws of the Holy Appurtenances: 30
Laws of *Birkat Hamazon:* 73

5. *Ben Ish Ḥay,* Shana Rishona — Laws of the Morning Blessing: Parashat Vayesheb

Laws of *Keriat Shema:* Parashat Shemot and Parashat Va'ere
Laws of the *Shemoneh Esre:* Parshiot Beshalaḥ: Terumah
Laws of Conduct in the Synagogue: Parashat Yitro
Laws of *Nesiyat Kapayim:* Parashat Teẓaveh
Laws of *Minḥa:* Parashat Vayakhel
Laws of *Birkat Hagomel:* Parashat Ekeb
Laws of *Arbit:* Parashat Pekudei
Sanctity of the Synagogue: Parashat Vayikra
Laws of *Birkat Hamazon:* Parashat Ḥukat

6. *Yalkut Meam Loez*

Laws of Morning Blessings: Bereshit Alef: 116
Laws of *Keriat Shema:* Debarim Alef: 375–387; Debarim Bet: 528, 577–78
Laws of the *Shemoneh Esre:* Debarim Bet: 536–538

Laws of Reading the Torah: Debarim Bet: 542; Bereshit Alef: 37; Debarim Dalet: 1427
Laws of *Aron Hakodesh:* Shemot Gimmel: 957
Laws of Conduct in the Synagogue: Bamidbar: 42, 43; Bereshit Bet: 729, 563; Shemot Gimmel: 1003
Laws of *Nesiyat Kapayim:* Bamidbar: 58–64
Laws of *Birkat Hagomel:* Bereshit Alef: 348; Shemot Alef: 359
Laws of *Birkat Hamazon:* Debarim Bet: 467
Laws of *Minḥa:* Bereshit Bet: 504
Laws of *Arbit:* Bereshit Bet: 555

Questions for Class Review or Homework Assignment

1. Name all the officials or officiants of a Sephardic synagogue, including its religious personnel, leaders of religious services, and congregational officers.
2. By what names is the special plaque of a *menorah,* which is at the front of most Sephardic synagogues, called? Explain why it has those names.
3. Name all of the major religious objects in a synagogue sanctuary. Name all of the religious appurtenances of the Sefer Torah as well.
4. What is the custom regarding the distribution of *aliyot* in your community?
5. Name the different types of prayerbooks used in your congregation throughout the year for the various occasions.
6. What are the most honored *aliyot* according to your tradition, and which of these is given to the rabbi?
7. Describe all the occasions on which they say *Birkat Kohanim* according to your tradition.

Topics for Class Discussion

1. What are the general obligations of a member or worshipper towards the synagogue?

2. Who sponsors the synagogue in your community? Describe the structure of the administration, how the synagogue policies are developed, etc.
3. What is the halakhic source for the "auctioning" of the *aliyot* and other *mizvot*, and how do you regard this system?
4. How do you compare decorum of your synagogue with that of other groups of Sephardim and with those of the Ashkenazim?
5. Discuss the customs of *Birkat Kohanim* which are different from those of Ashkenazim regarding frequency, removal of shoes, or hand-washing.

Shabbat

PART IV — CHAPTER 11

Basic Sources

For an overview of the Halakhah relating to the topics generally covered in this unit, it is suggested that the teacher review the following basic sources which can also be distributed as assignments for advance preparation of the subject matter.

1. *Shulḥan Arukh, Oraḥ Ḥayyim,* Vol. I

    Preparations in Honor of Shabbat: 242, 249–251, 253, 254, 256–258
    Welcoming the Shabbat — Candle-Lighting: 260–264
    Friday Evening Services: 267, 269, 270
    Friday Evening Home Ceremonies: 271–274
    Sabbath Morning in Synagogue and Home: 282, 285–287, 289, 290
    Seudah Shelishit: 291
    Shabbat *Minḥa:* 292
    Mozaei Shabbat in Synagogue and Home: 293–298, 300
    Special Shabbat Observances: 302, 319

2. *Kaf Haḥayyim,* Vol. IV: Same chapters as in *Shulḥan Arukh,* listed above.

3. *Mekor Ḥayyim Hashalem,* Vol. III

    Basic Concepts of Shabbat: 103, 104
    Preparations in Honor of Shabbat: 107, 108
    Welcoming the Shabbat — Candle-Lighting: 110–112
    Friday Evening Services in Synagogue and Home: 113–117
    Shabbat Morning in Synagogue and Home: 118, 120, 122,

123, 128–132, 134, 135
Shabbat *Minḥa — Seudah Shelishit:* 136
Moẓaei Shabbat in Synagogue and Home: 137, 138
Special Sabbath Observances: 147, 176

4. *Kiẓur Shulḥan Arukh Hashalem,* Vol. I

Preparations in Honor of Shabbat: 123, 130
Friday Evening Services in Synagogue and Home: 134, 139, 141, 142, 144
Welcoming the Shabbat — Candle-Lighting: 135, 136
Shabbat Morning in Synagogue and Home: 153–155, 157, 158
Seudah Shelishit: 159
Shabbat *Minḥa:* 160
Moẓaei Shabbat in Synagogue and Home: 161–165, 168
Special Shabbat Observances: 170

5. *Ben Ish Ḥay,* Shana Shenia

Kiddush: Bereshit
Candle-Lighting: Noaḥ
Preparations in Honor of Shabbat: Lekh Lekha
Welcoming the Shabbat — Friday Evening Home Service: Vayera
Shabbat *Minḥa — Seudah Shelishit:* Ḥayei Sarah
Shabbat Morning in Synagogue: Toldot
Moẓaei Shabbat in Synagogue and Home: Vayeẓe
Special Shabbat Observances: Vayeḥi

6. *Yalkut Meam Loez*

Welcoming the Shabbat: Bereshit Alef: 137–138
Special Shabbat Foods: Bereshit Alef: 141
Seudah Shelishit: Bereshit Alef: 143; Shemot Alef: 381
Kiddush: Shemot Bet: 588–594
Preparations in Honor of Shabbat: Shemot Bet: 407, 634; Shemot Gimmel: 1213
Shabbat Day in Synagogue and Home: Shemot Gimmel: 1105, 1208, 1209

Questions for Review or Homework Assignment

1. Describe the differences in emphasis in the preparation for Shabbat of any two groups. Include candle-lighting customs.
2. What are the differences in the recitation of *Kiddush,* both on Friday evening and Shabbat day? What is the most unique *Kiddush*?
3. What are some of the different foods enjoyed on the Sabbath day?
4. How is the study of Torah emphasized in connection with Shabbat?
5. What are the different kinds of "fourth meal" as relates to Shabbat?
6. What are some of the reasons for the customs relating to *Habdalah*?

Topics for Class Discussion

1. Why do some synagogues no longer recite *Kiddush* at the Friday evening services? Do the changes in our society relate to this problem?
   (See *Yeḥave Daat,* vol. 2, question 35 for background.)
2. Is the study of the weekly portion *Shenayim mikra ve'eḥad targum* still relevant when so many no longer understand the Aramaic? Would not the substitution of a translation into the vernacular be most appropriate for a better understanding of the Bible?
   (See *Yeḥave Daat,* vol. 2, question 37 for background.)
3. What special considerations should a Sephardi or Ashkenazi bear in mind when inviting a guest for Shabbat from the other group?

Pesaḥ, Lag LaOmer

PART IV — CHAPTER 12

Basic Sources

For an overview of the Halakhah relating to the topics generally covered in this unit, it is suggested that the teacher review the following basic sources which can also be distributed as assignments for advance preparation of the subject matter.

1. *Shulḥan Arukh, Oraḥ Ḥayyim*

   Shabbat Hagadol: 430
   Bedikat Ḥameẓ and *Biur Ḥameẓ:* 431–435, 439, 440, 443–445
   Making Utensils Kasher: 451, 452
   Laws of the *Maẓẓah:* 453, 454, 456, 458, 460–462
   Taanit Bekhorot: 470
   The Seder: 472–481
   Passover Services: 487–491
   Counting of the *Omer:* 489, 493
   Lag LaOmer: 493

2. *Kaf Ḥahayyim* — Same chapters as in *Shulḥan Arukh,* listed above

3. *Mekor Ḥayyim Hashalem,* Vol. IV

   Shabbat Hagadol: 182
   Ḥameẓ and *Maẓẓah:* 183, 185
   Bedikat Ḥameẓ and *Biur Ḥameẓ:* 184
   Making Utensils Kasher: 186
   Ereb Pesaḥ: 187
   Preparation of the Seder: 188
   Passover Services: 189, 192–194
   Laws of the Seder: 190, 191

Counting of the *Omer:* 195
Lag LaOmer: 195

4. *Kiẓur Shulḥan Arukh Hashalem,* Vol. II

 Shabbat Hagadol: 2
 Bedikat Ḥameẓ and *Biur Ḥameẓ:* 3–8
 Making Utensils Kasher: 22, 23
 Laws of the *Maẓẓah:* 24, 25, 27, 29, 33
 Taanit Bekhorot: 40
 The Seder: 42–51
 Passover Services: 57–61
 The Counting of the *Omer:* 59, 63
 Lag LaOmer: 63

5. *Ben Ish Ḥay* — The Laws of Pesaḥ, Shana Rishona, Parashat Ẓav

6. *Yalkut Meam Loez*

 The Seder, Shemot Alef: 233
 Taanit Bekhorot and Ereb Pesaḥ, Shemot Alef: 164, 200, 201
 Lag LaOmer, Parashat Bereshit Bet: 576

Questions for Review or Homework Assignment

1. What distinct differences are there in the recitation of the *Hallel* on Pesaḥ that can be discerned between all Sephardim and the Ashkenazim?
2. What difference is there in the blessings over the wine at the Passover home service (called "Seder" or "Haggadah")?
3. What customs do most Sephardim enact, at the early portion of the Pesaḥ home service, which are completely omitted by Ashkenazim?
4. What is the difference in the order of the Four Questions? Do all Sephardim have the same text for the Four Questions?
5. Do all Sephardim eat rice on Pesaḥ? If not, why not?

6. How many cups of wine do Sephardim pour at the Seder or Haggadah? Compare this with the Ashkenazim and explain the difference.
7. In what way is the Counting of the *Omer* of the Sephardim different from that of the Ashkenazim?

Topics for Class Discussion

1. Why do you think the Sephardim did not forbid *kitniyyot* on Pesaḥ?
2. How should Ashkenazim respond to the invitation of Sephardim for the Passover meals? What differences can be expected in the menu? May an Ashkenazi be present, considering these differences? (See *Yabia Omer* 5:37)
3. What connection is there between the Fifth Cup, which is for Elijah the Prophet, and the opening of the door for Elijah at the concluding portion of the Seder (or Haggadah) when we recite *Shefokh ḥamatekha al hagoyim*? (See *Keter Shem Tob,* Vol. 3, p. 186.)
4. Of what significance is it for some Sephardim to be given salt on the second night of Pesaḥ when they begin to count the *Omer?* What is salt considered as a *segula* for?

Yom Haaẓmaut, Shabuot
PART IV — CHAPTER 13

Basic Sources

For an overview of the Halakhah relating to the topics generally covered in this unit, it is suggested that the teacher review the following basic sources which can also be distributed as assignments to students for advance preparation of the subject matter.

1. *Shulḥan Arukh, Oraḥ Ḥayyim*

   Laws of Shabuot: 494

2. *Kaf Haḥayyim,* Vol. VI: Same chapters as in *Shulḥan Arukh,* listed above

3. *Mekor Ḥayyim Hashalem,* Vol. IV

   Laws of Shabuot: 196

4. *Kiẓur Shulḥan Arukh Hashelem,* Vol. II

   Laws of Shabuot: 64

5. *Ben Ish Ḥay*

   Laws of Shabuot, Shana Rishona, Parashat Bamidbar

6. *Yalkut Meam Loez*

   Shemot Bet — Laws of Shabuot: 883
   Debarim Bet: 685
   Eve of Shabuot: Debarim Bet: 532

Questions for Review or Homework Assignments

1. Describe a basic difference in the preparation of *ḥallot* for Shabuot.

2. What are the topics of Torah learning traditionally studied on Leil Shabuot?
3. What are some of the special customs relating to the types of foods served on Shabuot and the reasons for those customs?
4. What are the *Azharot*? Who wrote them, and when are they recited by the different groups of Sephardim?
5. What procedure is followed regarding the reading of *Megillat Rut*?

Topics for Class Discussion

1. Why do some groups stand and others sit for the reading of the Ten Commandments? (See *Yeḥave Daat,* Vol. 1, chapter 19.)
2. How does *Megillat Rut* represent the essence of Shabuot?
3. *Azharot* are said by some Sephardim on the Shabbat before Rosh Hashanah, the Shabbat after Rosh Hashanah (Shabbat Teshuba), and on the Shabbat before Pesaḥ (Shabbat Hagadol). What is the possible connection between these customs and the recitation of *Azharot* on Shabuot?
4. Ashkenazim do not recite *Azharot,* even though there were about ten different versions of these poetic prayers composed by such greats as Saadia Gaon, Naḥmanides, Shelomo ben Yehuda Gabirol, and Isaac Kimḥi. What do they chant on Shabuot which is not included in the Sephardic liturgy? Why is there such disparity in these particular customs? (See *Keter Shem Tob,* Vol. 4, p. 19.)

Tisha BeAb

PART IV — CHAPTER 14

Basic Sources

For an overview of the Halakhah relating to the topics generally covered in this unit, it is suggested that the teacher review the following basic sources which can also be distributed as assignments to students for advance preparation of the subject matter.

1. *Shulḥan Arukh, Oraḥ Ḥayyim,* Vol. II

   The Four Fast-Days: 549
   The Week in Which Tisha BeAb Falls: 551
   Ereb Tisha BeAb: 552
   The Meal Before the Fast: 553
   Forbidden Acts on Tisha BeAb: 554
   Laws of *Tefillin* and *Ẓiẓit* on Tisha BeAb: 555
   The Night and Day after Tisha BeAb: 558
   Laws of a Public Fast-Day: 566, 580
   Private Fast-Days: 578

2. *Kaf Haḥayyim,* Vol. VII — Same chapters as in *Shulḥan Arukh,* listed above

3. *Mekor Ḥayyim Hashalem,* Vol. IV

   Laws of Tisha BeAb and the Other Fast-Days: 202
   The Three Weeks: 203
   Forbidden Acts on Tisha BeAb: 204
   Prayers of Tisha BeAb and Its Customs: 205
   The Reasons for the Various Fasts: 206
   Laws of a Public and Private Fast: 207

4. *Kiẓur Shulḥan Arukh Hashalem,* Vol. II

   Laws of the Four Fasts: 117

Distinctions Between Tisha BeAb and the Other Fasts: 118
The Week in Which Tisha BeAb Falls: 119
The Laws of Tisha BeAb: 120
The Meal Before the Fast: 121
Forbidden Acts on Tisha BeAb: 122
Laws of *Ẓiẓit* and *Tefillin* on Tisha BeAb: 124
Laws of Night and Day after Tisha BeAb: 125

5. *Ben Ish Ḥay* — Laws of Tisha BeAb — Shana Rishona — Parashat Debarim

6. *Yalkut Meam Loez*

   Laws of Fast-Days, Debarim Alef: 309
   Laws of Tisha BeAb, Bereshit Bet: 560; Debarim Alef: 264
   Ereb Tisha BeAb: 301
   Forbidden Acts on Tisha BeAb, Debarim Alef: 305

Questions for Review or Homework Assignment

1. What is the *Mah Nishtanah* of Tisha BeAb?
2. What is the special announcement made by the rabbi, *Shimau na aḥeinu Bet Yisrael,* on the Eve of Tisha BeAb?
3. How many times does one put on *tefillin* on a fast-day? Are there any exceptions?
4. What prayer which is said by Ashkenazim on Yom Kippur is said by Sephardim on Tisha BeAb?
5. When must one refrain from eating meat before Tisha BeAb according to your tradition and one other tradition?
6. Describe the differences in the physical appearance of the synagogue on Tisha BeAb.

Topics for Class Discussion

1. Why do you think that all the fast-days (except possibly Tisha BeAb) were announced in synagogue on the Sabbath

before the week on which they occurred?
(See *Keter Shem Tob,* Vol. 5, p. 48)

2. Is it proper to put on *tefillin* on Tisha BeAb morning, and what is the rationale for your viewpoint?
(See *Yaḥave Daat,* Vol. II, chapter 67.)

3. Why do you think it is the custom not to say the blessing *Al mikra megillah* over *Eikha* just as we do over *Megillat Ester*?
(See *Keter Shem Tob,* Vol. V, p. 77.)

4. There is an interesting custom among the Egyptian Jews wherein all those who are called to the Torah on Tisha BeAb morning must be the same three called again at *Minḥa* on Tisha BeAb. Can you explain why?
(See *Keter Shem Tob,* Vol. V, p. 39.)

5. Can you imagine the reason for the Jews of Algeria to blow ten blasts of the *shofar* at the end of Tisha BeAb?
(See *Keter Shem Tob,* Vol. V, p. 62.)

Rosh Ḥodesh

PART IV — CHAPTER 15

Basic Sources

For an overview of the Halakhah relating to the topics generally covered in this unit, it is suggested that the teacher review the following basic sources which can also be distributed as assignments for advance preparation of the subject matter.

1. *Shulḥan Arukh, Oraḥ Ḥayyim*

   Work Customs: 417
   Fasting: 418
   Special Meal: 419
   Rosh Ḥodesh Services: 421–425
   Sanctification of the Moon: 426
   Rosh Ḥodesh Elul: 581

2. *Kaf Haḥayyim,* Same chapters as in *Shulḥan Arukh,* listed above

3. *Mekor Ḥayyim Hashalem,* Vol. IV

   Fasting on Ereb Rosh Ḥodesh: 177
   Work Customs—Special Meal: 178
   Rosh Ḥodesh Services: 179, 180
   Ṣanctification of the Moon: 181
   Rosh Ḥodesh Elul: 209

4. *Kiẓur Shulḥan Arukh Hashalem,* Vol. I

   Blessing the New Moon—Fasting—Work Customs: 251
   Special Meals: 253
   Rosh Ḥodesh Services: 255–257
   Sanctification of the Moon: 259
   Rosh Ḥodesh Elul: Vol. 2, chapter 146

5. *Ben Ish Ḥay*

   Laws of Rosh Ḥodesh, Sanctification of the Moon: Shana Shenia, Parashat Vayikra

6. *Yalkut Meam Loez*

   Blessing of the New Moon: Shemot Alef: 141
   Work Customs: Bamidbar: 343
   Rosh Ḥodesh Services: Bamidbar: 341
   Rosh Ḥodesh Elul: Debarim Bet: 513

Questions for Review or Homework Assignment

1. Why is Rosh Ḥodesh considered to be the special festival of the women?
2. Explain the difference in the usage of the blessing before the *Hallel* for Rosh Ḥodesh, as compared to the Three Festivals.

Rosh Ḥodesh Elul

1. What is the custom relating to the saying of the *Seliḥot* and the blowing of the *shofar* during *Ḥodesh Elul*?
2. What is the custom regarding the *Haftarah* when Rosh Ḥodesh Elul falls on Shabbat?

Topics for Class Discussion

1. In regard to the institution of the Hebrew calendar, why are some Rosh Ḥodesh celebrations for two days and some only for one day?
2. Discuss the significance of Ereb Rosh Ḥodesh being called Yom Kippur Katan.
3. Why don't the Sephardim announce the time of the *molad*, and why do they say, *Besiman tob yehei lanu Rosh Ḥodesh*?

Rosh Hashanah

PART IV — CHAPTER 16

Basic Sources

For an overview of the Halakhah relating to the topics generally covered in this unit, it is suggested that the teacher review the following basic sources which can also be distributed as assignments for advance preparation of the subject matter.

1. *Shulḥan Arukh, Oraḥ Ḥayyim*

   Service in Synagogue and Home on Rosh Hashanah and *Aseret Yemei Teshuba:* 582–584, 598, 599, 601, 601
   The *Musaf* and Blowing of the *Shofar* on Rosh Hashanah: 585, 586, 588, 590, 591, 596

2. *Kaf Haḥayyim* — Same chapters as in *Shulḥan Arukh,* listed above

3. *Mekor Ḥayyim Hashalem,* Vol. IV

   Rosh Hashanah Services: 218-226 and 235-238
   Blowing of the *Shofar:* 227–235
   Aseret Yemei Teshuba: 239–243

4. *Kiẓur Shulḥan Arukh Hashalem,* Vol. II

   Rosh Hashanah and *Aseret Yemei Teshuba* Services in Synagogue and Home: 147–149, 157, 163–166
   Blowing of the *Shofar:* 150, 151, 153, 155, 161

5. *Ben Ish Ḥay* — Laws of Rosh Hashanah, Shana Rishona, Parashat Niẓabim

6. *Yalkut Meam Loez,* Bamidbar: 343

Questions for Review or Homework Assignment

1. Explain the symbolism of as many foods as you can which are used in connection with the *Yehi razon* prayers on the first night.
2. What are some special prayers in your Rosh Hashanah service which are different from those of other Sephardim?
3. Describe the order of the *shofar*-blowing ceremony and the number of *shofar* sounds. Compare this with one other group which conducts these ceremonies in a different manner.
4. What is the special service held on the afternoon of Rosh Hashanah called, and how is it observed?

Topics for Class Discussion

1. What should be the qualifications for the *ḥazzan* on the High Holy Days?
2. What kind of posture in prayer and voice is considered appropriate in the *Yamim Noraim* services?
3. What different attitudes are expressed by whether or not one should wear new clothes on Rosh Hashanah?
4. Why do Sephardim not say *Sheheḥeyanu* on the second day of Rosh Hashanah?

Yom Kippur

PART IV — CHAPTER 17

Basic Sources

For an overview of the Halakhah relating to the topics generally covered in this unit, it is suggested that the teacher review the following basic sources which can also be distributed as assignments to students for advance preparation of the subject matter.

1. *Shulḥan Arukh, Oraḥ Ḥayyim*

   Ereb Yom Kippur—Laws and Customs: 604–608
   Candle-Lighting: 610
   Yom Kippur Services: 619, 622–624

2. *Kaf Haḥayyim* — Same chapters as in *Shulḥan Arukh,* listed above

3. *Mekor Ḥayyim Hashalem,* Vol. IV

   Ereb Yom Kippur—Laws and Customs: 252–254
   Yom Kippur Services: 262–273

4. *Kiẓur Shulḥan Arukh Hashalem,* Vol. II

   Ereb Yom Kippur—Laws and Customs: 168–172
   Candle-Lighting: 174
   Yom Kippur Services: 183–188

5. *Ben Ish Ḥay* — Laws of Yom Kippur, Shana Rishona, Parashat Vayelekh

6. *Yalkut Meam Loez—Miẓvot* of Yom Kippur: Vayikra: 288–289

Questions for Review or Homework Assignment

1. Describe the manner in which the *Kapparot* ceremony is regarded in your community and in one other.
2. Why and how is the book of *Tehillim* studied on Rosh Hashanah and Yom Kippur?
3. At what time is the *shofar* blown to conclude the *Neilah* service, and what is the sequence of *shofar* blasts?
4. When is *Al ken nekaveh* said by all Sephardim?
5. How is the bowing down in the *Musaf* enacted by the congregation?
6. What relationship do the *Ḥatan Bereshit* and *Ḥatan Torah* have to Yom Kippur?

Topics for Class Discussion

1. Describe the historical background of *Kal Nidrei* and how it is recited differently among the Sephardim.
2. How would you justify the concept of "auctioning off" Torah honors in the synagogue as a democratic procedure?
3. Describe the significance of the kindling of lights on Yom Kippur, and show how it affects the solemnity of the day.

Sukkot, Shemini Ḥag Haaẓeret, Simḥat Torah

PART IV — CHAPTER 18

Basic Sources

For an overview of the Halakhah relating to the topics generally covered in this unit, it is suggested that the teacher review the following basic sources which can also be distributed as assignments to students for advance preparation of the subject matter.

1. *Shulḥan Arukh, Oraḥ Ḥayyim*

    General Laws: 625
    Dwelling in *Sukkah:* 639
    First Day of Sukkot on Shabbat: 642
    Kiddush: 643
    Hallel: 644
    Laws of *Lulab:* 645
    Hadas: 646
    Araba: 647
    Etrog: 648
    Blessing Over *Lulab:* 651
    Time for Blessing *Lulab:* 662
    Lulab on First Day: 658
    Torah Readings: 659
    Hakkafot: 660
    Kiddush, Second Night: 661
    Order of Service, Second Day: 662
    Hoshaana Rabba: 664
    Sukkah on Seventh Day: 666
    Shemini Ḥag Ha-aẓeret: 668
    Simḥat Torah: 669

2. *Kaf Haḥayyim* — Same chapters as in *Shulḥan Arukh*, listed above

3. *Mekor Ḥayyim Hashalem,* Vol IV

Laws of *Sukkah:* 220
Night of Sukkot and Laws of Dwelling in *Sukkah:* 221
The *Arba'ah Minim:* 222
Order of Services and Taking of *Lulab:* 223
Hoshaanah Rabba: 224
Shemini Ḥag Ha-aẓeret and Simḥat Torah: 22

4. *Kiẓur Shulḥan Arukh Hashalem,* Vol. I

Laws of *Sukkah:* 189
Sekhakh: 192
Dwelling in *Sukkah:* 202
Kiddush: 206
Hallel: 207
Lulab: 208
Hadas: 209
Araba: 210, 213
Taking *Lulab:* 214, 215
Taking *Lulab* on First Day: 221
Torah Reading: 222
Hakkafot: 223
Second Day of Festival: 224, 225
Hoshaana Rabba: 227
Sukkah on Seventh Day: 229
Shemini Ḥag Ha-aẓeret: 308
Simḥat Torah: 309

5. *Ben Ish Ḥay*—Laws of Sukkot: Shana Rishona, Parashat Ha'azinu, Hoshaana Rabba, Simḥat Torah, Parashat Vezot Haberakha

6. *Yalkut Meam Loez*

Laws of *Sukkah:* Vayikra: 296
Dwelling in *Sukkah:* Vayikra: 295, 297

Nisukh Mayim: Bamidbar: 346, 347
The Festival of Sukkot: Debarim Bet: 686
Shemini Ḥag Ha-aẓeret: Bamidbar: 345
Simḥat Torah: Shemot Bet: 920

Questions for Review or Homework Assignment

1. What are some of the decorations placed in the *sukkah* according to your tradition and according to that of one other group?
2. What provision does your community make to enable those who do not have their own *sukkah* to observe the festival properly?
3. What is the order of the waving of the *lulab,* and what does it symbolize?
4. Describe the observance of Hoshaana Rabba and tell when (and if) the *shofar* is blown on that day.
5. How do you prepare the *arba'ah minim* according to your tradition, and how does it differ from one other group?
6. What do you do with the *arba'ah minim* after Sukkot?
7. What is your congregation's custom regarding *Hakkafot* on Simḥat Torah evening or on the following day? How is this different from one other group's customs?
8. What honors and obligations relate to *Ḥatan Torah* and *Ḥatan Bereshit*?

Topics for Class Discussion

1. What should be the demeanor in the synagogue on Simḥat Torah? Should the occasion be a solemn one, or should there be special license to express joy in ways that would not normally take place in the synagogue?
2. How does the Halakhah relate to women regarding those commandments for which they are not obligated, such as *lulab* and *sukkah*? Is a blessing made by women on such commandments?

3. There are different customs as to when the *Mashib haruaḥ* is said on Shemini Ḥag Ha-aẓeret. What is the significance of mentioning the blessing for the rain specifically then, after Sukkot has already ended?
4. Explain the reasons for the Torah's requirement to move into a "temporary dwelling" for Sukkot. Also, discuss the significance of celebrating Sukkot in the month of Tishri, when, in reality, Sukkot commemorates the encampment of the Jews in the desert in Nisan after *Yeẓiat Miẓrayim*.

Ḥanukkah

PART IV — CHAPTER 19

Basic Sources

For an overview of the Halakhah relating to the topics generally covered in this unit, it is suggested that the teacher review the following basic sources which can also be distributed as assignments to students for advance preparation of the subject matter.

1. *Shulḥan Arukh, Oraḥ Ḥayyim*

   Laws of *Menorah* Lighting: 671, 672, 676, 678–680
   Ḥanukkah Services in Synagogue and Home: 670, 682–684

2. *Kaf Haḥayyim* — Same chapters as in *Shulḥan Arukh,* listed above

3. *Mekor Ḥayyim Hashalem,* Vol. IV

   Historical Background of Ḥanukkah: 226
   Menorah Lighting Laws: 227
   Ḥanukkah Services in Synagogue and Home: 228

4. *Kiẓur Shulḥan Arukh Hashalem,* Vol. II

   Laws of Candle-Lighting: 234, 235, 239, 241–244
   Ḥanukkah Services in Synagogue and Home: 233, 245–247

5. *Ben Ish Ḥay*—Laws of Ḥanukkah: Shana Rishona, Parashat Vayeshev

6. *Yalkut Meam Loez*—Laws of Ḥanukkah: Bamidbar: 101

Questions for Review or Homework Assignment

1. What are the different versions of the blessing over the candles?
2. What is the purpose of the *shamash*?
3. Describe special foods eaten on Ḥanukkah.
4. What special traditions relating to the collecting of *ẓedakah* were enacted by the children on Ḥanukkah?
5. Why are the words *Mizmor shir ḥanukkat habayit LeDavid* omitted in the daily Sabbath and festival services, except on Ḥanukkah?
6. What is the *Shir shel yom* for Ḥanukkah?
7. What is Shabbat Hahalbashah?
8. What kind of *Ḥanukkiyyot* are used by the different groups of Sephardic Jews?

Topics for Class Discussion

1. Can an electric *ḥanukkiyya* be used to fulfill the *miẓvah* of lighting the Ḥanukkah lights?
2. From an historic and halakhic point of view, how are women featured as part of the Ḥanukkah celebration, and what ramifications follow in regard to their recitation of the *Hallel?*
3. Is the giving of gifts a part of the Ḥanukkah tradition among the Sephardim?
4. Why is the emphasis of the miracle of Ḥanukkah attached to the "pitcher of oil" rather than to the victory of the Maccabees?
5. What is the reason that Ḥanukkah was not established to be celebrated for nine days (as is done on other holidays due to uncertainties in the Jewish calendar)?

Tu BiShebat and Shabbat Shira

PART IV — CHAPTER 20

Basic Sources

For an overview of the Halakhah relating to the topics generally covered in this unit, it is suggested that the teacher review the following basic sources which can also be distributed as assignments to students for advance preparation of the subject matter.

1. *Mekor Ḥayyim Hashalem,* Vol. IV

   Laws of Tu BiShebat, chap. 229

2. *Yalkut Meam Loez*

   Tu BiShebat: Rosh Hashanah Le'ilanot: Debarim Bet: 649

3. *Peri Eẓ Hadar*—Customs of Tu BiShebat

4. *Sefer HaToda'ah,* Customs of Tu BiShebat, p. 213

5. *Talmud,* Masekhet *Rosh Hashanah,* 2a, Mishna 1 provides source of observance of Tu BiShebat

Questions for Review or Homework Assignment

1. What are the *arba kosot* of Tu BiShebat?
2. Why do we celebrate Tu BiShebat, and what are its sources?
3. What are the various names of Tu BiShebat?
4. How is Tu BiShebat observed in Israel today?
5. What are the home ceremonies in the observance of Tu BiShebat?

Topics for Class Discussion

1. Show how Tu BiShebat represents the notion that it is incumbent upon man to reap the utmost of pleasure from the world around him, which is the opposite of asceticism.
2. What special customs relate to the singing of *Az Yashir Moshe*?

Purim

PART IV — CHAPTER 21

Basic Sources

For an overview of the Halakhah relating to the topics generally covered in this unit, it is suggested that the teacher review the following basic sources which can also be distributed as assignments to students for advance preparation of the subject matter.

1. *Shulḥan Arukh, Oraḥ Ḥayyim*

    The Fast of Esther: 686
    Laws of *Megillah*: 687–692
    Purim Customs in Synagogue and Home: 693–695, 697

2. *Kaf Haḥayyim* — Same chapters as in *Shulḥan Arukh,* listed above

3. *Mekor Ḥayyim Hashalem,* Vol. IV

    The Fast of Esther: 231
    Megillah Reading: 232
    Purim Customs in Synagogue and Home: 234

4. *Kiẓur Shulḥan Arukh Hashalem,* Vol. II

    The Fast of Esther: 249
    Megillah Reading: 250, 252, 253, 255
    Purim Customs in Synagogue and Home: 256–259

5. *Ben Ish Ḥay* — Laws of Purim, Shana Shenia, Parashat Teẓave

6. *Yalkut Meam Loez,* Megillat Ester

    Purim Laws: 254–262
    The Fast of Esther: 233, 262, 263, 302
    Laws of *Megillah:* 264, 265

Questions for Review or Homework Assignment

1. What special customs are observed in synagogue on the Shabbat before Purim?
2. How is the tradition of *mishloaḥ manot* enacted in your community?
3. What are the usual (or unusual) ways in which one fulfills the biblical command "to blot out the name of Amalek" on Purim?
4. Why do we contribute the *maḥaẓit hashekel* on the eve of Purim or on Purim day, and what specific law does this teach us in addition to the specific historic event(s) that this ceremony commemorates?
5. What are the specific laws regarding the poor on Purim, and how do we enact them?
6. Name some of the Purim delicacies for which your community is known. Is there any connection between these types of foods and the Purim story?
7. What are the laws of mourners in connection with Purim?

Topics for Class Discussion

1. How is the importance of the Jewish woman reflected in the observances prior to and during Purim?
2. It became the custom in Israel for cities in which the Jewish inhabitants were saved from some local disaster at the hands of their enemies to establish the day of victory as the "Purim" of their city. The famous story of the Purim of Saragossa (Spain), also called Purim de los Sargosonos (which coincides with Tu biShebat), is one such example. Can you describe any other such Purims?

3. What are the basic laws of Shushan Purim and how does one mark the day here? What special observances will appertain in certain cities of the State of Israel where you may someday visit during Purim?
4. What is meant by the saying, "a Purim gift given after Purim"? What are some of the Purim opportunities which come but once a year? What does this tell about the general quality of life that prevailed during the rest of the year?

For Further Reading, Reference, Viewing and Listening

Albertson, Charles, *American Sephardi Resource Guide,* Young Leadership Division, American Sephardi Federation, New York, 1987.

Angel, Marc D., *The Rhythms of Jewish Living: A Sephardic Approach,* Sepher-Hermon Press, Inc., for Sephardic House at Congregation Shearith Israel, New York, 1986.

La America: The Sephardic Experience in the United States, Jewish Publication Society of America, Philadelphis, 1982.

Angel, Gilda, *Sephardic Holiday Cooking,* Decalogue Books, Mount Vernon, New York, 1986.

Ashtor, Eliyahu, *The Jews of Moslem Spain,* Vol. III, Jewish Publication Society, Philadelphia, 1985.

Ben-Ami, Issachar, *The Sepharadi and Oriental Jewish Heritage Studies,* The Magnes Press, The Hebrew University, Jerusalem, 1982.

Benbassa, Esther, *Cuisine Judeo-Espagnole Recettes et Traditions,* Scribe, Paris, 1984.

Bitton, Rabbi David, *Siddur Kol Yaakob,* Daily Prayer Book according to the Minhag of Aleppo (Aram Ṣoba), Sephardic Heritage Foundation, Inc., New York, 1985.

Carciente, Jacob, *Apuntes Para La Historia De La Gran Sinagoga Tiferet Israel De Caracas,* Asociacion Israelita de Venezuela, 1980.

Cardozo, Abraham Lopes, *Sephardic Songs of Praise* (Tenu Shebaḥa Vegam Shira), Tara Publication, Cedarhurst, NY 1987 (plus cassette which includes 14 Zemirot accompanied by guitar and flute).

Cohen, Dr. Robert, *The Jewish Nation in Surinam*: Historical Essays, I. Emmering, Amsterdam, 1982.

Crespil, Marcel, *Mogador Mon Amour,* Vantage Press, New York, 1987.

De Felice, Renzo, *Jews in An Arab Land,* translated by Judith Roumani, University of Texas Press, Austin, 1985.

Deshen, Shlomo and Walter P. Zenner, eds, *Jewish Societies in the Middle East: Community, Culture and Authority,* University Press of America, Washington, D.C., 1982.

Dwek, Poopa, *Deal Delights,* Sisterhood of the Deal Synagogue, Deal, NJ, 1977.

Elazar, Daniel, Harriet Pass Friedenreich, Baruch Hazzan and Adina Weiss, *The Balkan Jewish Communities: Yugoslavia, Bulgaria, Greece and Turkey,* University Press of America, Lanham, MD, 1984.

Elbaz, Andre E., *Folktales of the Canadian Sephardim,* Fitzhenry and Whiteside, Toronto, 1982.

Freidenreich, Harriet Pass, *The Jews of Yugoslavia,* Jewish Publication Society, Philadelphia, 1979.

Gaon, Solomon and M. Mitchell Serels, *Sephardim and The Holocaust,* Yeshiva University, New York, 1987.

Grunwald, Max, *Tales, Songs and Folkways of Sephardic Jews,* Edited by Dov Noy, The Magnes Press, The Hebrew University, Jerusalem, 1982.

Ha-Cohen, Mordecai, *Higgid Mordecai,* The Story of Libya and Its Jews, (Hebrew) Institute Ben-Zvi, Research Center on The Jews of North Africa, Jerusalem, 1981.

Haddad, Heskel, *Jews of Arab and Islamic Countries: History, Problems, Solutions,* Shengold Publishers, New York, 1983.

Ha-Kohen, Mordecai, *The Book of Mordecai,* Institute for The Study of Human Issues, Philadelphia, 1980.

Halperin, Don A., *Old Synagogues of Turkey,* Wyndham Hall Press, Bristol, 1986.

Hillel, Shlomo, *Ruaḥ Kadim,* (Hebrew), Ministry of Defense, Tel Aviv, 1985.

The Jews in Morroco: Life, Customs and Art, (Hebrew), Stavit and Israel Museum, Jerusalem, 1984.

Juifs d'Egypte Images et Textes, Editions du Scribe, Paris, 1982.

Kalderon, Albert D., *Abraham Galante: A Biography,* Sepher Hermon Press, New York, 1983.

Kashani, Reuben, *Yahadut Bukhara,* (Hebrew), Brit Yoẓei Bukhara, Ḥebron Iẓuv, Jerusalem, 1973.

Illustrated Ketubot of Afghanistan, (Hebrew), Sephardi Council of Jerusalem, Jerusalem, 1978.

The Crypto-Jews of Mashad, (Hebrew), Sephardi Council of Jerusalem, and the Sephardi Department of the World Zionist Organization, Jerusalem, 1979.

The Jewish Communities in Egypt, (Hebrew), Sephardi Council of Jerusalem, Jerusalem, 1984.

The Jewish Communities in the Far East, (Hebrew), Sephardi Council of Jerusalem, and the Sephardi Department of the World Zionist Organization, Jerusalem, 1982.

The Jewish Communities in Persia-Iran, (Hebrew), Sephardi Council of Jerusalem, and the Sephardi Department of the World Zionist Organization, Jerusalem, 1979.

The Jewish Communities in Turkey (Hebrew), Sephardi Council of Jerusalem, Jerusalem, 1984.

Koen-Sarano, Matilda, *Kuento del Folklor de la Familiya,* Djudeo-Espanyola, (plus cassette), Kana, Jerusalem, 1986.

Laredo, Victor, *Sephardic Spain,* Editorial Mensaje, New York, 1978.

Laskier, Michael, M., *The Alliance Israélite Universelle and The Jewish Communities of Morocco, 1862–1962,* State University of New York Press, Albany, NY, 1983.

Levy, Emilie de Vidas, *Sephardic Cookery, Traditional Recipes for a Joyful Table,* Women's Division, Central Sephardic Jewish Community of America, Inc., New York, 1983.

Levy, Rebecca, Amado, *I Remember Rhodes,* Sepher Hermon Press for Sephardic House at Congregation Shearith Israel, New York, NY, 1987.

Lewis, Bernard, *The Jews of Islam,* Princeton University Press, Princeton, New Jersey, 1985.

Menasce, Elsie, *The Sephardi Culinary Tradition,* The Sephardic Cookbook Corporation Publishers UCA Studio (Pty) Limited, Cape Town, South Africa, 1984.

Mishal, Yisrael, *Between Afghanistan and Eretz Yisrael,* (Hebrew), Sephardi Council in Jerusalem, Jerusalem, 1982.

Marciano, Eliahu, *Ir Hakohanim Dubdo Marokko,* (Hebrew), published by the author, Jerusalem, 1987.

Papo, Joseph M., *Sephardim in Twentieth Century America: In Search of Unity,* Pelé Yoetz Books, San Jose, California and Judah L. Magnes Museum, Berkeley, Calilfornia, 1987.

Patai, Raphael, *The Vanished Worlds of Jewry,*MacMillan, New York, 1981.

PE'AMIM—Studies in the Cultural Heritage of Oriental Jewry, (Hebrew), Itzḥak Bezalel, Editor, Ben Zvi Institute for the Study of Jewish Communities in the East, Quarterly, numbers 1–32, Jerusalem, Spring 1979–1987.

Raphael, Chaim, *The Road from Babylon, The Story of Sephardi and Oriental Jews,* Harper & Row, New York, 1985.

Roumani, Maurice, *The Case of The Jews from Arab Countries,* WOJAC, Tel Aviv, 1983.

Sabar, Yona, *The Folk Literature of Kurdistani Jews,* (Yale Judaica Series; 23) Yale University Press, New Haven, 1982.

Seder Tefillat Haḥodesh, Sinai Publishing House, Tel Aviv, 1983.

Sitton, David, *Sephardi Communities in Our Days,* (Hebrew), Council of Sephardi and Oriental Communities, Jerusalem, 1982.

Sephardi Community Today, (translated from the Hebrew), Council of Sephardi and Oriental Communities, Hamakor Press Ltd., Jerusalem, 1985.

Stampfer, Judah, *The Sephardim: A Cultural Journey From Spain to the Pacific Coast,* Institute for Judaic Studies, Portland, Oregon, 1987.

Stillman, Norman A., *The Jews of Arab Lands: A History and Source Book,* Jewish Publication Society of America, Philadelphia, 1979.

Sutton, Joseph A. D., *Aleppo Chronicles: The Story of the Unique Sephardeem of the Ancient Near East—in Their Own Words,* Thayer Jacoby, Brooklyn, N.Y., 1987.

Tillem, Ivan L., *The 1987—88 Jewish Almanac,* Pacific Press, New York, 1987.

Toledano, Joseph, *Jewish Life in the Mellah,* Stavit, Jerusalem, 1984.

Weinberger, Leon J., *Bulgaria's Synagogue Poets: The Kastoreans,* Hebrew Union College Press, Cincinatti, 1983.

Ye'or, Bat, *The Dhimmi,* Farleigh Dickinson University Press and London and Toronto Associated University Presses, Rutherford, Madison and Teaneck, New Jersey, 1985.

Periodicals

The Alliance Review, The American Friends of Alliance Israélite Universelle Inc., Quarterly, New York.

Bama'aracha, Council of the Sephardi and Oriental Communities of Jerusalem, Monthly, Jerusalem, March, 1984.

Horizon Sephardi, Fédération Séphardie Canadienne, Monthly, Montreal, Quebec, June 1980.

La Voix Sépharade, Communauté Sépharade du Québec, Monthly, Montreal, Quebec, May 1983.

The Pedagogic Reporter, Jewish Education Service of North America, Inc., Quarterly, New York, 1987, Special Issue on Teaching About Sephardic Jewry, Vol XXXVII No. 1.

Sephardi Heritage, Council of the Sephardi and Oriental Communities, Quarterly, Jerusalem, Winter 1982.

Sephardi World, World Sephardi Federation, Sephardi Communities Department, World Zionist Organization, Bi-Monthly, Jerusalem, April-May 1984.

The Sephardic Connection, Young Leadership Division of the American Sephardi Federation, Quarterly, American Sephardi Federation, New York, Spring-Summer 1987 Vol. 6, No. 2.

The Sephardic Voice of America, Independent Newspaper, Monthly, Publisher, Rabbi Hanania Elbaz, Editor: Rabbi Elie Elbaz.

Films

Jews of Fez, 14 minutes, black and white, 1976, video cassette. Available from Jewish Media Service, Jewish Welfare Board, 15 East 26th Street, New York NY 10010–1579.

The Sephardi Experience, 29 minutes, color, 1978, 3/4 video cassette, cable TV only, available from Tarbuth Foundation, 129 West 67th Street, New York, NY 10023.

Sephardic Concert, by David Abikzer, 60 minutes, color, VHS video cassette. Accompanied by Kol Israel Orchestra. Ten classical Sephardic Selections. Available from Hed Artsi, P. O. Box 248, Woodmere, NY 11598.

The Song of the Sephardi, 75 minutes, color, 1978, produced by David Raphael of Los Angeles. Available from Jewish Media Service, Jewish Welfare Board, 15 East 26th Street, New York, NY 10010–1519. Film describes life and culture of Judeo-Spanish Jews in Seattle, Washington.

Surinam, 28 minutes, color, 1978, 3/4 video cassette cable TV only. Available from Tarbuth Foundation, 129 West 67th Street, New York, NY 10023.

Note: As of February, 1988, all films listed in this book as available from Jewish Media Service JWB, may only be secured from JESNA (Jewish Education Service of North America), Jewish Media Resource Network, Dr. Tamar Ariav, Director, 730 Broadway, N.Y., N.Y., 10003.

Cassettes

Abikzer. David

Sephardic High Holy Day Day Selections produced by CBS. Piyutim for the Yamim Noraim.

Sephardic Greatest Hits (Spanish and Hebrew) produced by House of Menorah, New York City.

Shirim Upiyoutim from the Book of "Shirei Yedidot", 3 cassettes of the songs and piyutim of Morrocan Jewry.

Zemirot Yisrael, Songs of the Edot Yisrael produced by Koliphone, Israel.

The Sephardic Shabbat with Louis E. Rousso singing the Bendicho in Judeo-Spanish by Hed Artsi.

All the above are available from Hed Artsi, P. O. Box 248, Woodmere, New York, NY 11598, or from Cantor David Abikzer, 706 Arbuckle Avenue, Woodmere, NY 11598.

Ben-Haim, Rabbi Abraham

Weekly Torah Readings (Parashiot) and Haftarot, Jerusalem Nusaḥ, with Hebrew derashot on each weekly sidrah. Available from Rabbi Ben-Haim, 5B Defoe Place, Co-op City, Bronx, NY 10475.

Cardozo, Abraham Lopes, *Sephardic Songs of Praise* (Tenu Shebaḥa Vegam Shira), Tara Publications, Cedarhurst, NY, 1987 (plus cassette which includes 14 zemirot accompanied by guitar and flute).

Levy, Cantor Meir, *Hello from New York,* Liturgical and Traditional Songs, Reuveni Brothers, Jerusalem, 1987. Available from Cantor Meir Levy, 2197 East 2nd Street, Brooklyn, NY 11223 or c/o Ahiezer Congregation, 1885 Ocean Parkway, Brooklyn, NY 11223.

Maimon, Rabbi Solomon

Hagaddah Shel Pesaḥ, in Hebrew and Ladino according to the Turkish liturgy. Accompanied by Explanatory Booklet.

Sephardic Traditions in the Synagogue and Home Segments of the liturgical services in the synagogues and the home in Hebrew and Ladino according to the Turkish liturgy. Accompanied by Explanatory Booklet. Both available from Rabbi Solomon Maimon, 7002 Seward Park Avenue South, Seattle, WA 98118.

Lekha Dodi Sephardic Shabbat Kit, prepared by Rabbi Marc D. Angel and narrated by Rabbi Abraham Ben-Haim. Cassette and Study Guide on the liturgy and customs of the Sabbath. Available from Sephardic House c/o Congregation Shearith Israel in the City of New York, 8 West 70th Street, New York, NY 10023.